C000196674

"These are fantastic: information and bea[t] inside a backpack"—**J**

"Dit is gebruikersvrie[n] opvoedkundige waarde

"Handy travel companions … these guides may be small but they're literally jam-packed with information … making these guides holiday must-haves for an informed and more enjoyable trip" —*Longevity* **magazine**

"These handy books are accessible to everyone from the lay person to geologists and scientists, answering all your questions regarding these sites"—*Saturday Dispatch*

"… compact pocket guides packed with info, maps and colourful pictures"—*50/50*

"They are a celebration of various aspects of South Africa[n] culture, including our historical inheritance and the land on which we live" —**Diane de Beer,** *Pretoria News*

"There's this marvellous new collection of pocket guides by Southbound, each highlighting a specific World Heritage Site in South Africa … Easy to use and fun to read, the pocket guides are a must for anyone remotely interested in our country's heritage" —*Independent on Saturday*

"These books reveal fascinating parts of our country that many of us aren't properly aware of. They'd make excellent gifts, singly or collectively, and are great primers for planning a holiday" —**Bruce Dennill,** *The Citizen*

"All [eight] of South Africa's World Heritage Sites are covered, each in a manageable pocket guide which provides a remarkable amount of information for the edification of the serious ecotourist … comprehensive contents … an extensive amount of information …" —**Carol Knoll,** *Environmental Management*

Also by David Fleminger:

Back Roads of the Cape (Jacana 2005)

The Cradle of Humankind (Southbound 2006)

Vredefort Dome (Southbound 2006, 2008)

Mapungubwe Cultural Landscape (Southbound 2006)

The Richtersveld Cultural and Botanical Landscape—including
Namaqualand (Southbound 2008)

Swaziland (Southbound 2009)

Lesotho (Southbound 2009)

Published in 2006, updated and reprinted in 2009 by
Southbound, an imprint of 30° South Publishers (Pty) Ltd.
28, Ninth Street, Newlands
Johannesburg 2092, South Africa
www.30degreessouth.co.za
info@30degreessouth.co.za

Design and origination by 30° South Publishers (Pty) Ltd.

Printed and bound by Pinetown Printers (Pty) Ltd.

Although the publishers and author have done their best to ensure that all
the facts contained in this pocket guide are accurate and up to date, they
accept no responsibility for any loss, injury or inconvenience caused to any
person, resulting from information contained herein.

ISBN 978-0-958489-12-6

Southbound Pocket Guides
to South Africa's
World Heritage Sites

Robben Island

David Fleminger

Revised and updated

South Africa's Eight World Heritage Sites

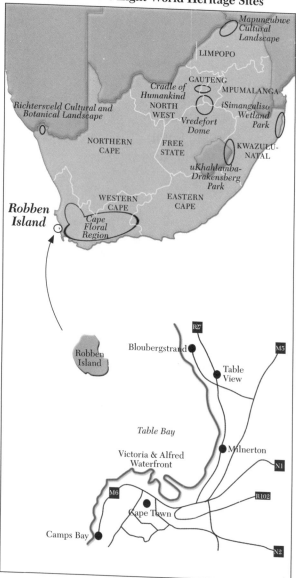

David Fleminger. Because of his passion for wandering the globe, travel writing appears to be evolving as a focus in David Fleminger's life. His first book, *Back Roads of the Cape*, was published in 2005. He is also author of five of the Southbound World Heritage Sites pocket guides—*Robben Island, Mapungubwe Cultural Landscape, The Cradle of Humankind, The Richtersveld Cultural and Botanical Landscape* and *Vredefort Dome*.

David has also worked in many different aspects of the media industry—as a script writer, director, editor, post-production supervisor, interviewer and producer. ("I am an avid movie watcher with an extensive knowledge of useless movie trivia.") He has written and directed theatre shows, TV series and educational videos and is studying for an MA in Tourism & Heritage Studies at Wits University.

A born-and-bred Joburger, he lives in the northern suburbs with sundry pets and housemates. He spends his time watching theatre, cricket and walking his dogs in the park.

The *Southbound* series of pocket guides celebrates South Africa's eight unique UNESCO World Heritage Sites:

- Robben Island
- iSimangaliso Wetland Park (formerly Greater St. Lucia Wetland Park)
- uKhahlamba-Drakensberg Park
- Mapungubwe Cultural Landscape
- Cape Floral Region Protected Areas
- The Cradle of Humankind
- Vredefort Dome
- The Richtersveld Cultural and Botanical landscape (including Namaqualand)

1. What is UNESCO and the World Heritage List? 8
UNESCO and Robben Island 11
Where is it? 13

2. Early history 15
The seafarers 15
The first prisoners – Xhore and John Crosse 16
The Dutch arrive 20
Van Riebeeck, Autshumao and Krotoa 21
Robben Island under the Dutch 30
The British, the Dutch and Napoleon's war 33
The Anglo-Xhosa wars 36
The second generation 38
Lepers and lunatics 43
The military years 51

3. The Apartheid years 56
Prison life and prison resistance 63

4. Exclusive interview 72
Matlakana Philemon Tefu—former political
prisoner incarcerated on Robben Island from
1964 to 1985

5. Fauna and flora 81

6. Map of Robben Island 83

7. Visiting Robben Island 84
The V&A Waterfront 84
The Nelson Mandela Gateway 85
The ferry ride 87
The bus tour 89
The prison tour 93
A walking tour of Robben Island 97
Final thoughts 101

8. The site today 102
   Plans for the future 102
   Robben Island Museum information 103

9. References/further reading 106
   Useful websites 107

Index 108

Acknowledgments 112

Contents

What is UNESCO and the World Heritage List?

UNESCO (United Nations Economic, Scientific and Cultural Organization) was formed shortly after the World War II when it was realized that, as a species, we don't really get along. The newly formed United Nations therefore set up an organization which would promote co-operation between nations by sharing knowledge and promoting culture. But, after the horror of two world wars in which millions of lives and many irreplaceable global resources were lost, it became apparent that building classrooms, mounting festivals and publishing scientific papers that no one would read was not enough. So, the UN charged this specialized agency with a very ambitious goal—to build peace in the minds of men (and presumably women too).

But that's not all. To quote from UNESCO's most recent manifesto, the organization 'is working to create the conditions for genuine dialogue based upon respect for shared values and the dignity of each civilization and culture. This role is critical, particularly in the face of terrorism, which constitutes an attack against humanity. The world urgently requires global visions of sustainable development based upon observance of human rights, mutual respect and the alleviation of poverty, all of which lie at the heart of UNESCO's mission and activities.'

In 1972, this mandate was significantly enlarged at the *Convention concerning the Protection and Preservation of World Cultural and Natural Sites*. The original impetus for this worthy endeavour came about several decades earlier because, as is often the case, a valuable site was about to be destroyed in the name of progress. In this instance, it was the Abu Simbel temples in Egypt, which were going to be flooded by the soon-to-be-completed Aswan Dam. The year was 1959 and, thanks to international pressure and funding, the threatened temples were quickly dismantled and re-assembled out of harm's way before the damn dam was built.

Soon, authorities in charge of other endangered sites applied to the UN for protection and assistance and, in 1965, the United States proposed a 'World Heritage Trust' that would 'identify, promote and protect the world's superb natural and scenic areas and historic sites for the present and the future of the entire world citizenry.' In 1968, the International Union for Conservation of Nature (IUCN) developed similar proposals for its members and, eventually, a single text was agreed upon by all parties concerned, which resulted in the adoption of the abovementioned convention of 1972.

So, if Bird flu, global warming and nuclear Armageddon don't get us, UNESCO is working, along with its 190 member states, to make sure that our precious heritage resources are maintained for future generations. As UNESCO acutely points out, 'by regarding heritage as both cultural and natural, the Convention reminds us of the ways in which people interact with nature, and of the fundamental need to preserve the balance between the two.'

That's good news, and the World Heritage List is growing. Every year, additional sites are proposed by local stakeholders to the central committee. A team of investigators is then sent out to write a report on each nominated site. After studying these independent reports, the committee finally selects several lucky applicants to be inducted onto the list. Since South Africa ratified the World Heritage Convention in 1997, we have become particularly well-endowed in this regard. We already have eight sites on the list, quite a large number considering the relatively small size of our country and the short time we have been back in the UN fold since the dark days of international isolation.

Furthermore, our sites are biologically diverse and historically significant, offering the planet crucial lessons about tolerance, conservation and nation-building.

Highlights of the Convention protecting world cultural and natural heritage

The General Conference of the United Nations Educational, Scientific and Cultural Organization meeting in Paris from 17 October to 21 November 1972, at its seventeenth session,

Noting that the cultural heritage and the natural heritage are increasingly threatened with destruction not only by the traditional causes of decay but also by changing social and economic conditions which aggravate the situation with even more formidable phenomena of damage or destruction,

Considering that deterioration or disappearance of any item of the cultural or natural heritage constitutes a harmful impoverishment of the heritage of all the nations of the world,

Considering that protection of this heritage at the national level often remains incomplete because of the scale of the resources which it requires and of the insufficient economic, scientific, and technological resources of the country where the property to be protected is situated,

Considering that parts of the cultural or natural heritage are of outstanding interest and therefore need to be preserved as part of the world heritage of mankind as a whole,

Considering that, in view of the magnitude and gravity of the new dangers threatening them, it is incumbent on the international community as a whole to participate in the protection of the cultural and natural heritage of outstanding universal value, by the granting of collective assistance which, although not taking the place of action by the State concerned, will serve as an efficient complement thereto,

Having decided, at its sixteenth session, that this question should be made the subject of an international convention,

Adopts this sixteenth day of November 1972 this Convention.

UNESCO and Robben Island

It's obvious why Robben Island is important to South Africans. For over 500 years, this little nugget of rock has been a staccato counterpoint to the country's history; a melancholy echo of every significant event that took place on the mainland. It was a pantry for the early European seafarers, who stocked up on seals and penguins before continuing on their treacherous journey to the East. The Dutch used it as a place of banishment for unruly 'citizens'. The British used it as a prison for intransigent Xhosa chiefs who were causing trouble on the eastern frontier. It has also been used as a leper asylum, a mental asylum, a military base during World War II and, most famously, as a place to isolate the political agitators fighting the apartheid state.

Robben Island is therefore many things to many people, but there is a common thread running through the island's history. For centuries, it has served as a place to put the unwanted members of society—people that the authorities would rather have out of sight and out of mind. However, nothing about the island is clear-cut. In their analysis of the island, the International Council on Monuments and Sites (ICOMOS) expert mission admitted that 'it is difficult to find an exact parallel for Robben Island among the penitentiary islands of the period of European colonization. Norfolk Island off the coast of Australia was used for criminals transported from Britain in the nineteenth century and Devil's Island off the coast of French Guyana served a similar purpose, while the island of Alcatraz in San Francisco Bay is the archetypal convict island, but none of these filled the political role of Robben Island under Dutch and British colonial rule, and in particular in the later twentieth century.'

The long history of the island notwithstanding, the first thing most people think of when they hear 'Robben Island' is Nelson Mandela, and this is fair enough. Our beloved Madiba has certainly left his mark on Robben Island and vice versa. But, while the star-power of Mandela tends to overwhelm the island, it should always be remembered that it was not only populated by ANC cadres. Apart from the Khoikhoi and Xhosa resistance leaders of previous centuries, as a twentieth-century political prison, it held representatives of the PAC (Pan Africanist Congress, headed by Robert Sobukwe), SWAPO (the South West African People's Organization, headed by Herman Toivo ya Toivo) and dozens of other labour organizations and liberation movements, all of whom played their parts in challenging and eventually defeating the monstrous system of apartheid.

More importantly, Robben Island has now transformed itself into a potent symbol of the 'New South Africa', a miraculous country, characterized by tolerance, forgiveness and triumph over terrible odds. As Ahmed Kathrada stated when the island first became a museum in 1996, "While we will not forget the brutality of apartheid, we will not want Robben Island to be a monument of our hardship and suffering. We would want it to be a triumph of the human spirit against the forces of evil; a triumph of wisdom and largeness of spirit against small-minded pettiness; a triumph of courage and determination over human frailty and weakness."

And therein lies the importance of Robben Island, both for the people of South Africa and citizens of the world. As the Nomination Committee declared in their submission to UNESCO, "Robben Island has come to represent an outstanding example of a symbol representing the physical embodiment of the triumph of the human spirit over enormous adversity and hardship. The role of Robben Island in the transformation of an oppressed society has come to symbolize the rebirth of democracy in South Africa, a country which has come to be viewed as a unique example of transformation in a world troubled by political uncertainty."

For all of these reasons, and many others too subtle to enumerate, Robben Island became World Heritage Site number 916 in 1999, under criteria iii and iv, viz:

iii. to bear a unique or at least exceptional testimony to a cultural tradition or to a civilization which is living or which has disappeared;

iv. to be an outstanding example of a type of building, architectural or technological ensemble or landscape which illustrates (a) significant stage(s) in human history.

Today, Robben Island is a National Heritage site and all property and buildings are owned by the state, including a buffer zone of one nautical mile around the island. The only exception to this is the Church of the Good Shepherd, which is owned by the Church of the Province of South Africa. A Robben Island Council has been set up to oversee policy and financial issues, while the on-site management has been delegated to the director of the Robben Island Museum and its staff. National Works Department and National Ports Authority staffs are also active on the island.

Where is it?

Robben Island is located a short distance off the coast of Cape Town. It is within sight of Table Bay, Bloubergstrand, Sea Point and Camps Bay, and it is clearly visible from the top of Table Mountain. It is situated about ten kilometres from the V&A Waterfront, and about seven kilometres from the beach at Bloubergstrand. Despite its close proximity to Cape Town, the island is naturally isolated from the mainland by a short but formidable stretch of cold, wild ocean. It is this paradoxical combination of remoteness and accessibility that made Robben Island such a useful prison.

The highest point on the island is Minto Hill, about 30 metres above sea level, and there is an attractive lighthouse standing atop this low rise. The depth of the sea between Robben Island and the mainland is also about 30 metres and the island is actually joined to the mainland by a submerged saddle of land. In earlier times, when the sea level was lower, this saddle may have been exposed and it is possible that our early ancestors lived on the island. It is also possible that, in more recent times, the native Khoikhoi paddled across the seas and frequented the island in the years before the white man came. Thus far, no archaeological evidence has been found to support either of these conjectures.

Physically, the kidney-shaped island is about two and a half kilometres from east to west and about three kilometres from north to south, giving it a total area of 574 hectares. It is about 12 kilometres in circumference. Walking along the perimeter road (as I was privileged enough to do) is an incredibly rewarding experience—but more about that later in the book.

The seas around the island are notoriously rough and, to make matters worse, the island is surrounded by a fearsome barricade of jagged rocks that stretches out into the dark-green water. Combine this with the fierce winds and thick fog which can roll in off the Atlantic and you have a recipe for shipwrecks on a grand scale. Even though they used to light signal fires on top of Fire Hill (now called Minto Hill), over 30 shipwrecks have been recorded on the shores of this tiny outcrop. About two thirds of these occurred before the lighthouse was built in 1863, but ships continue to be surprised by the island. The northern shore boasts the remains of at least three recent shipwrecks, all rusting away on the serrated rocks.

Researchers at the University of Cape Town are currently mapping and studying the island's shipwrecks, but the rough sea conditions make them difficult to locate and investigate. Dr. Bruno Werz, a pioneer in this study, has even proposed that the water around the island be declared an archaeological reserve to protect the wrecks and to preserve any precious relics which they may harbour.

Early History

The seafarers

I am loath to start the island's story with the arrival of the Europeans. It makes me feel like one of those old-school historians who began every book with the arrival of Jan van Riebeeck. However, in this case, it may be appropriate.

Although archaeological research is still on-going, there is little evidence to suggest that the indigenous people of the Cape ever bothered to paddle across the rough seas to the island. But it must have been tantalizing; being so close to an untouched island, crawling with colonies of fat seals and juicy penguins, yet unable to reach it.

In fact, it was these unfortunate sea creatures that initially defined the island, making it a useful stop for hungry European sailors on their way to the East. They would regularly drop anchor here to harvest a boatload of seals and penguins. Records state that sailors could herd up to 1,100 penguins in a single day. Indeed, the island's current name comes from the Dutch word *robbe* which means 'seal'.

The first recorded mention of the island is by Vasco da Gama, the Portuguese explorer who helped pioneer the sea route around the Cape. He stopped on the island in 1496 to collect seals for meat and oil. As the volume of shipping picked up from the 1500s onward, many more European seafarers chose to anchor off the island to replenish their stores. They seemed to prefer the uninhabited rock to the mainland, which was populated by the potentially hostile Khoikhoi people.

The Khoikhoi had cattle, however, and the seafarers needed to trade with the Khoikhoi to replenish their meat stocks. But relations between the two were tempestuous. Neither group ever understood what the other was saying and the Europeans tended to be rather aggressive in their bartering. After a memorable skirmish with a pompous Spanish admiral, in which several Europeans lost their lives, the Khoikhoi were generally given a wide berth.

So, the first role of Robben Island was as a storehouse or larder for the European seafarers. Several captains even left sheep and goats on the island so that they would breed, and thus supply them with fresh meat when they returned months later. Unfortunately, these flocks were often picked up by other ships instead, and it was difficult to keep track of the various herds that somehow managed to eke out an existence on the little island. Dassies (large but cute rodents, more correctly known as a hyrax or coney) were also brought in from Dassen Island.

From the 1600s onward, the Europeans used the island as an informal post office, leaving letters and reports under specially marked 'post-office stones' for allied ships that came calling. There are also several reports of shipwrecked sailors who were forced to live on the island for months at a time, while waiting to be rescued.

The first prisoners – Xhore and John Crosse

For 150 years, the various European nations jostled with each other to assume dominance of the lucrative sea route to the East. In 1602, however, the Dutch East India Company (the VOC—*Vereenigde Oost-Indische Compagnie*) was formed in Holland. This determined little corporation, the first limited stock company in the world, made it their capitalistic duty to secure control over the route to the East, a valuable trade network that brought exotic spices (such as pepper, nutmeg and cloves) to Europe from what is now Malaysia and Indonesia. The VOC 'capital' was in Jakarta

To support this enterprise, the VOC started investigating the establishment of a permanent European presence at the strategic Cape of Good Hope, situated halfway between the Old the New Worlds. This is a position the Cape still holds today, geographically and metaphorically. But the Dutch weren't the only people to consider this. In fact, the first real attempt to start a settlement at the Cape was undertaken by the VOC's rivals, the British East India Company, in 1614. The plan was to send 100 convicts to the Cape each year, allow them to negotiate with the local tribes and hope that they could establish a base for British interests. Whoever thought that a group of hardened criminals would make for effective diplomats was clearly an idiot and the plan ended in disaster. It all began with a Khoikhoi chief called Xhore (or Coree) who was resident at Table Bay (then called Saldania) in the early seventeenth century. In 1613, Xhore and a companion were on board a British ship called the *Hector*, trading with the captain. Suddenly, the *Hector* hauled anchor and sailed away. It is unclear whether this was an accidental or intentional kidnapping, but there is evidence to suggest that Sir Thomas Smythe (the founder of the British East India Company and a very powerful merchant) planned the whole thing. He wanted to get his hands on one of the incomprehensible Khoikhoi locals in order to teach him the Queen's English and inculcate him as a British agent.

In any event, the unfortunate Khoikhoi passengers must have been extremely anxious as the strange 'water-dwelling' sailed away from the African coast. The ship's log tells of hunger strikes by the 'honoured guests' and Xhore's companion died at sea. Once in London, Xhore was treated as visiting royalty and lived with the eminent Sir Thomas Smythe for six months. He may have even met with King James but the glories of Britannia were not enough to win over the reluctant tourist. Unsurprisingly, the first English words that Xhore learned were along the lines of 'I want to go home!'.

Sir Thomas eventually relented and put Xhore back on the *Hector* the next time it sailed for the East. The voyage was fraught with storms and close calls, but the relieved chief was eventually deposited back on his home soil. Once reunited with his people, a grateful Xhore was quick to implement the lessons he had learned in London and immediately put his prices up. Iron hoops and copper were no longer deemed desirable and sheets of brass were now required before the Khoikhoi would part with any of their livestock.

Nevertheless, the British Empire was built on large ideas and narrow minds and Smythe persisted with his plans to establish a British presence at the Cape.

Finding his company strapped for cash, however, Smythe couldn't afford any reputable colonists. Unperturbed, he perused the prisoners being held at Newgate Prison and offered a motley group of ruffians and bounders the choice of being hanged for their crimes or sent as ambassadors to the wild Cape of Storms. Smythe, ever a man of principle, refused to consider anyone accused of rape, burglary or witchcraft.

An assortment of 18 or 19 men was duly selected and sent to the Cape instead of the gallows. They were the first group of prisoners to be 'transported', a practice that later became quite common and would eventually culminate in the Australian nation.

It appears that only ten convicts finally disembarked at the Cape in 1615. The others either escaped en route, continued onto the Indies or died from scurvy. The new settlers chose as their leader the particularly aggressive and rebellious Captain John Crosse. He was a 'gentleman' who had lost his post in the King's Guard as a result of his fondness for duelling and subsequently became a renegade highwayman.

They were thus abandoned at the Cape with 'something for his own defence against wild beasts and men, weapons and victuals'. They were also left a small rowboat. But things quickly went wrong.

The first Crosse-led British deputation to Xhore resulted in a skirmish in which several men were killed or injured. This was described as a 'misunderstanding' by Xhore who wanted to know why the British had left people behind to live on Khoikhoi land. He offered to help the settlers only if England would support him in his conflict with the inland tribes. A short time later, there was another more serious clash between the ex-con settlers and Xhore's people, and this forced the white men to jump into their little boat and flee to Robben Island. According to one contemporary account, Captain Crosse died in this altercation. Another account states that he made it to Robben Island.

Nine months after the convicts had first been deposited, the *New Year's Gift* landed at the Cape. When the landing party met with Xhore, he calmly informed them that several white men were living on Robben Island. When a rescue party went to the island they found only six survivors.

It later came to light that the refugees, who had somehow managed to survive on an island with few trees and almost no fresh water, had seen the *Gift* idling out at sea and grew impatient for their rescue. Several men tried to sail a raft, made from their wrecked rowboat, over to their would-be saviours. A whale unfortunately chose this moment to surface and overturned the raft, drowning some men. The others made it back to the island and a second attempt was made, possibly by Crosse alone. This time, contrary tides swept the raft out to sea and no further sightings of John Crosse were ever recorded.

Three of the survivors decided to remain on the island rather than return to England and they may or may not have been subsequently rescued by a Dutch or Portuguese ship. The other three chose to face the music back home and went aboard the *New Year's Gift*. Their time on the island had done nothing to reform the criminals, however, and the behaviour of the rescued men on board the *Gift* was declared so 'lewd' that they were often put into the ship's stocks as punishment. Within hours of their landing in England, the incorrigible convicts had stolen a purse and were 'executed upon their former condemnation, for which they were banished … but never pardoned'. Talk about delaying the inevitable.

Xhore, for his part, never received a reply to his request for assistance against his enemies and presumably determined that the Europeans were a bunch of rotters. This low opinion was confirmed in 1625, when Xhore was killed by a group of disgruntled Dutch traders. After his death, Xhore's sons inherited his distrust of the white man and were instrumental in the first Khoikhoi–Dutch war of 1658 (about which more later).

Towards the end of the seventeenth century, Xhore's Gorachouqua tribe migrated inland. They are thought to have established the Kora (or Koranna) tribe which was to battle with the Boer ancestors of the Dutch in the 1800s. As Mark Twain said, "History doesn't repeat itself, but it does rhyme."

The Dutch arrive

After the disastrous English attempt to settle at the Cape, the Europeans were much more circumspect in their ambitions (although Thomas Smythe did try to settle another three convicts at the Cape a short time later, before finally giving up the whole idea as a bloody waste of time).

Then, as every apartheid-era school kid knows, in 1652, a former ship's surgeon named Jan van Riebeeck was sent by the Dutch East India Company to establish a permanent refreshment station at the Cape. The purpose of this enterprise was to supply the ships that stopped at the Cape with fresh fruit, vegetables, water and meat—all at a healthy profit of course. To do this, however, the new settlers would have to cultivate a vegetable garden and negotiate with the local Khoikhoi for cattle and sheep.

On the surface, this may look like a fool's errand and it could have been just another anecdotal episode in the annals of European history. However, the Dutch were serious about their mission and spent months getting everything ready. In due course, three ships set sail, carrying 150 men and a few women to their new lives at the Cape. It was to be the beginning of a great South African drama that would span the next three and a half centuries.

Van Riebeeck, Autshumao and Krotoa

When Van Riebeeck arrived, he had many things to do. He had to build shelter for his fellow VOC employees. He had to establish trading links with the local people (whom the European's despised as violent, Godless and dirty). He had to establish a vegetable garden and cultivate European plants in an alien land (a task which fell to head gardener Hendrik Boom). And he had a wife, Maria, and an infant son who had travelled with him to a dangerous land far across the seas.

It wasn't going to be easy. But Van Riebeeck was determined to prove himself to the mighty VOC. He was, after all, a middle-manager who sought promotion—he had already been reprimanded in his previous post when he was caught trading for his own benefit.

For the first few years, the Dutch settlement at the Cape struggled. They managed to build a small fort with mud walls but they did not always have enough food to feed the men and women in the garrison. More often than not, they bought supplies from the ships in the bay instead of the other way round.

The local Khoikhoi (whom the European's dismissively called the Hottentots, apparently because of a refrain they chanted while dancing) didn't help. They were justifiably wary of the arrogant white men with straight hair who had come in magical ships that sailed on the water, and were reluctant to barter cattle and food with them.

As a result of their impoverished living conditions, Van Riebeeck often had to send small boats to Robben Island to collect seals and penguins to feed the fort. In fact, there was so much seal slaughtering going on during the seventeenth and eighteenth centuries, the clever seals left Robben Island and established new colonies on less accessible islands along the West Coast. To date, the seals have not yet returned to Robben Island in great numbers but it is hoped that a colony will re-establish itself now that the wildlife is protected. So, when you next see seals playing in the calm waters of Murray Harbour at Robben Island, tell them that it's safe to return …

Still, man cannot live by penguins alone and, in order to survive, Van Riebeeck needed the support of the local Khoikhoi tribes: the Goringhaiqua, the Gorachouqua, the Chainouqua, the Chochoqua and the Goringhaikona. It was the Goringhaikona, called the Strandlopers (beachcombers) by the Dutch, who lived in the immediate vicinity of Table Bay. As such, they bore the brunt of the new settlers' ambitions.

The Strandlopers were a lowly lot—a ragtag bunch of individuals thrown together by circumstance, rather than a cohesive tribal group. They had few cattle or goats and many members of the group were refugees from other tribes. As a result of their mongrel status, they were often picked on by other tribes and their small flocks were constantly raided by more powerful chiefs. At the time of Van Riebeeck's landing, the Strandlopers were reduced to gathering roots and scavenging food along the tide line.

The ersatz leader of the Strandlopers was Autshumao (also spelt Autshumato) and, in many ways, his story is the sequel to that of Xhore. It begins in 1631, before Van Riebeeck's arrival, when Autshumao was taken to Batavia by the British and taught rudimentary English. Once again, the Brits were hoping to 'civilize' Autshumao, whom they re-named Harry, so that he could act as an agent between the British and the Khoikhoi tribes at the Cape.

When he returned, however, the English discovered that Harry was nowhere near as popular with his fellow Khoikhoi as they would have liked him to be. A dispute between the tribes soon arose and Harry apparently requested that he and 20 followers be relocated to Robben Island where they would be safe from the stronger, predatory tribes who lived on the mainland. His duties on the island included acting as a postman and lighting the signal fire on Fire Hill (Minto Hill) to warn ships which would otherwise have crashed onto the dark island. Over the next decade or two, Harry and his followers regularly asked to be taken from the island to the mainland and back again, as their needs dictated.

By this time, Harry had become quite fond of the British. They called him King Harry and afforded him respect, responsibility and some livestock. Unfortunately, the ships that brought the first permanent settlers to the Cape were Dutch, not British. Nevertheless, Harry stepped forward as the chief of the Goringhaikona and addressed the chief Dutchman in English. Van Riebeeck could speak some English and the two embattled leaders soon formed a shaky allegiance which was based on necessity rather than trust.

During the first few weeks of their arrival, the VOC employees got busy building a fort and defences. Van Riebeeck put the word out that he wished to barter for cattle and goats, and wanted to live in peace with the local tribes. But the high walls of their new fort and the defensive moat that gaped below indicated otherwise—and at no time did the Dutch ask for permission to live on the Khoikhoi's land. Consequently, negotiations with the Khoikhoi were tricky and livestock was often withheld from the Dutch, despite their enticing offers of tobacco and strong spirits.

For his part, Van Riebeeck wrote in his journal that it

would have been much easier to take the cattle by force and enslave the local population. Company policy, however, was to make friends with the local tribes and Van Riebeeck's mercenary instincts were kept in check. Just how the Company intended their commander to keep the peace while simultaneously usurping the land without any kind of permission or payment, is not recorded.

Autshumao, who was now referred to as 'Herrie' by the Dutch, realized both the danger and the potential of the predicament in which he was caught. He was the only one who could speak a European language, albeit imperfectly, and he longed to improve his standing and the status of his tribe. Facilitating trade between the Khoikhoi and the Dutch could make him rich and powerful, and promises of tobacco, arrack, copper and beads were tempting. But he still didn't trust the pale-faced long-hairs ...

Another major character now enters the story. Krotoa was Autshumao's young niece who had been effectively orphaned when her father died and her mother went off to marry a more powerful chief. Krotoa was about nine years old when the Dutch landed and, although it is not quite clear how it transpired, Krotoa soon began living at the fort to help Maria van Riebeeck with her young son, Lambertus. Maria may have requested assistance, Autshumao may have asked the Van Riebeecks to take in his sickly niece, or the wily Chief Herrie may have engineered the situation to get someone inside the fort who could report back to him about the strange new people living on his beach. In any event, Krotoa was re-named Eva by the Dutch and began to learn the language, religion and strange ways of the Europeans.

As time passed, the Dutch settlement grew larger and their small flocks began to swell. Autshumao was worried that the *!uri-khoi* (white men) were too strong. Other peninsular tribes also became increasingly anxious as the Dutch took over more and more of their traditional grazing land. Autshumao's plan to become a power broker in the region was falling apart.

Krotoa was also having difficulty with her split allegiance. To the Khoikhoi she was the Dutchman's slave. To the Dutchmen she was still an untrustworthy native. As her mastery of Dutch improved, however, she started translating for Van Riebeeck and eventually unseated Autshumao from his position as interpreter. Her honest and innocent replies were much appreciated by the Dutch after Herrie's unreliable and shrewd interpretations, but this made 'Eva' even more unpopular with her own people.

As she developed into her teens, Krotoa found herself in an unenviable position. She longed for acceptance from two mutually incompatible cultures and wanted everyone to live together in harmony. But she could not fully appreciate the monumental consequences of the events going on around her. It is also likely that she started seeing the Khoikhoi through the condescending and dismissive eyes of the Europeans, and began to doubt her own traditions and self-worth.

Chief among her Khoikhoi detractors was Doman. He was a member of the more powerful Goringhaiqua tribe and, like Autshumao, Doman contrived to ingratiate himself with the Europeans while simultaneously questioning their motives. Due to his seemingly pious demeanour, he was nicknamed 'Dominee' (priest) by the Dutch and taken to the East for further instruction. When he returned, he understood the Dutch only too well and soon became a political agitator for their removal. While he kept up the appearance of servitude to Van Riebeeck, even renaming himself Anthony, Doman repeatedly warned his people that the Dutch were going to take over. They had already usurped all the grazing land around the peninsula, and would not stop until they had enslaved the Khoikhoi—just as they had done to the Malays. Doman blamed Autshumao for allowing the Dutch to become so strong and was particularly scathing about Krotoa for betraying her own people.

Autshumao decided that things had gone far enough. He had to act like a chief. So, at around the time that Van

Riebeeck's second son was born, the Strandlopers stole the company cattle and absconded into the interior, taking Eva with them. Unfortunately, the young European boy herding the flocks was killed in the raid. This further infuriated the Dutch. Fearful of reprisals, Eva was ordered not to return to the fort and for several weeks she was kept as a virtual captive.

The Dutch, however, were in no position to be indignant. They needed the support of the local people to survive and sent word that all would be forgiven if the cattle were returned. Finally, Eva managed to slip away and returned to the fort but she was unable to shed light on where the cattle were being kept. Autshumao, for his part, did not receive the hero's welcome he had expected from the other Khoikhoi tribes and he eventually returned to the fort with a peace offering of 40 cows, which he traded with the Dutch on behalf of an inland tribe.

Autshumao vehemently denied any involvement in the cattle theft and murder, but Doman and other members of the Goringhaiqua fingered Herrie as the culprit. Herrie was consequently exiled to Robben Island along with two fellow Khoikhoi, named Jan Cou and Boubou. By this time, the island already had an overseer and a small boat, the *Schapenjacht*, was periodically sent over with supplies. Apart from that, however, the prisoners were pretty much left to fend for themselves. Herrie became very depressed and lethargic. Eva also became distressed at the dire fate that had befallen her uncle and guardian.

Furthermore, Eva was finding it extremely difficult to navigate her way through the fraught politics between local tribes and the intractable Europeans. The brutal adult world of international relations must have been very confusing for the teenager who was still trying to forge her own personal identity. One account has it that, in her middle teens, Eva began to despair of ever finding a Khoikhoi husband and was made pregnant by a passing French sailor. To make

Southbound Guide to South Africa's World Heritage Sites

matters worse, she was developing a taste for alcohol, which was liberally used in all negotiations with the Khoikhoi. This insidious drug was to dog her throughout her later years.

By 1658, relations with the Khoikhoi had deteriorated to such a degree that an open rebellion broke out. This is now somewhat grandly called the First Khoikhoi–Dutch War, but it was really a series of skirmishes and raids on the Dutch positions. It was instigated by Doman and Osinghkhimma, the rebellious son of Gogosoa—the ageing 'Fat Captain' of the Goringhaiqua. This 'war' is said to be the first instance of organized resistance to white rule in South Africa.

During these hostilities, Herrie was fetched from the island to see if he could defuse the situation. He was either unwilling or unable to help and was sent back to his barren domain in the sea. The old chief was a determined man, however, and perhaps emboldened by the rebellion, he and an accomplice managed to steal a leaky boat and rowed themselves back to the mainland. Herrie immediately disappeared into the interior and only emerged from hiding many months later. His subsequent role in the Khoikhoi resistance movement is difficult to determine but he did earn himself a place in history as the first person to escape from Robben Island.

The rebellion continued until 1660, when European guns and Doman's injury in a fight took the wind out of the resistance. Doman, Herrie and the local chiefs realized that they would have to sue for peace. Eva presided at the final peace talks, in which Van Riebeeck dismissed the Khoikhoi's request to get their grazing land back. He said that the peninsula now rightfully belonged to the Dutch by means of conquest. After all, the Khoikhoi had started the war and the Dutch were going to keep the land for which they had fought. Clearly, the Christian edict to behave unto others as you would have them behave unto you was easily forgotten, especially when dealing with beastly heathens.

As the bearer of such bad news, Eva found herself even

more alienated from her people and she realized that her position as Van Riebeeck's interpreter had changed her life forever. Autshumao was also affected by the devastating result of the negotiations and was understandably reluctant to resume his position as a cattle broker for the Dutch. He lived out the rest of his days in relative obscurity and died in 1663 at an advanced but indeterminate age.

Another important man in Eva's life landed at the Cape in 1659. He was a young Danish citizen named Pieter van Meerhof, who had come to the Cape to find adventure and fortune. Although officially a soldier, he had some previous medical training and his services were soon in demand by the struggling community of Company employees. Van Meerhof also proved himself to be a good explorer, accompanying and eventually leading several expeditions into Namaqualand. The purpose of these journeys was to locate Monomatapa—the fabled city of gold; home to a wealthy civilization which had been integral to European lore on Africa for over a century. Little did they know that the Kingdom of Monomatapa was far to the north, toward the Zambezi River, and contained little mineral wealth.

Although they didn't find a city of gold in the Northern Cape, they did find the Namaqua people and Van Meerhof is credited with winning their trust and initiating diplomatic relations with this feared tribe. Back home, he and Eva also initiated 'diplomatic relations' and Eva became pregnant with Van Meerhof's child. Contrary to the norms of the time, Pieter acknowledged his baby and announced his intention to marry Eva. This shocked the Dutch as much as it did the Khoikhoi.

Back in Holland, the VOC was very disapproving but Van Meerhof was insistent. Then, to compound the problem, Eva fell pregnant again. At the same time, the Van Riebeecks announced that they were leaving the Cape for Batavia, where Jan had secured a new post. Eva was deeply upset that her 'second family' was about to depart but, before they left, they arranged for Eva's children to be baptised and helped pave the way for her unpopular marriage. Accordingly, Van Riebeeck's successor was instructed by the Company to allow the two to marry before they had any more little bastards.

At first, things seemed quite good for Eva and Pieter. He was rising through the Company ranks and Eva finally had a family of her own. Then, Pieter was appointed as the new overseer of Robben Island, which by now had quite a few prisoners (both Khoikhoi and European) who had fallen foul of the Company's draconian rules. Much to her dismay, Eva and her three children had no choice but to follow Pieter to the inhospitable island. In fact, this may well have been the reason why Pieter and his half-caste brood were transferred off the mainland in the first place.

Life must have been very lonely for Eva on Robben Island. She had no support apart from Pieter and found herself making friends with the Khoikhoi prisoners. When the moon was full, she would often dance with them and share their alcohol (which was occasionally earned in exchange for working on Company projects). Pieter was infuriated whenever she left the children to dance on the beach with her brethren and he once pushed the drunken Eva onto the floor, fracturing her skull. Nevertheless, they repeatedly worked out their problems and continued to live on the island for three long years.

Finally, Pieter got his chance for promotion when he was appointed to lead a slaving expedition to Madagascar to pick up some human cargo for the Company. Unsurprisingly, the Malagasy natives were less than thrilled to see the slaving party land on their shores, and Pieter was killed in the Bay of Antongill in 1667.

Eva was now a widow and returned to the mainland. Sadly, she was a shadow of her former self, broken by years of loneliness and a severe identity crisis. Most of the people she had known had died or left the Cape. She was spurned by the Khoikhoi and ignored by the Dutch. She began to drink heavily and spent nights away from her children, sleeping rough on the beach. Finally, the commander of the settlement took her children away from her and gave them to the head of the church. Eva fell apart. She became a public nuisance and was sent to Robben Island again, this time as a prisoner.

Her last years were repetitively tragic. Whenever she was released from the island, her drinking would land her in trouble again and she would be sent back. She fell pregnant several times by undisclosed men and her children were taken away from her as soon as they were born. She reformed and relapsed so many times that she became a figure of ridicule and disgust. Krotoa was finally released from her earthbound purgatory when she 'quenched the fire of her sensuality by death' in 1674, at the age of 31.

The story of Herrie, Eva and the first ten years of the Dutch settlement at the Cape are often touching, sometimes funny and frequently tragic. They speak to us as human beings and they resonate with ambiguous lessons about identity, culture, honour, loyalty and betrayal. The tale also highlights two of the first personalities to be closely associated with Robben Island. As such, Eva and Herrie deserve commemoration and remembrance. Sadly, this hasn't happened in any substantial way. Until recently, one of the ferries that carried visitors to and from the island was named in Autshumao's honour, but this vessel has now been decommissioned. Krotoa/Eva, meanwhile, has never had any significant memorial. One hopes that this omission will be rectified, as she can rightfully claim to be Robben Island's first martyr and one of the most poignant casualties of that initial meeting between black and white at the Cape.

Robben Island under the Dutch

As has been mentioned previously, Robben Island served a variety of purposes over the years and it was a useful place for the Dutch settlers. They made periodic visits to harvest seals and penguins, until the depredation of the native wildlife (once described as 'wondrous') became so widespread that it resulted in the one of the first conservation orders in South Africa. This edict stated that the island's seals and penguins could only be harvested under permit. To enforce this decree, an overseer was sent to the island. The first post-holder was Corporal Robbeljaert. Shepherds were also placed there to protect the small flocks of sheep and goats from hungry sailors who might steal the animals, to avoid paying the premium of buying their supplies from the refreshment station at Table Bay.

In 1654, as the flocks grew, several men were sent to the island to build shelters and plant a vegetable garden. The island slowly evolved into a small community that cultivated what the famous botanist Carl Thunberg declared to be the finest cauliflowers in the world! Large quantities of sea shells were discovered on the island and were used to manufacture lime. Outcrops of good limestone and Malmesbury slate were also identified.

The first official group of prisoners was sent to the island in 1657 and put to work quarrying this stone, which was used to build houses and roads in the fledgling settlement of Cape Town. This group of errant slaves and exiles did not prove to be a satisfactory work force, however, and the company had similar difficulty in finding competent overseers who could bear to live on the desolate isle. Sickness and hunger stalked these early inhabitants but the livestock flourished and, by 1666, the island boasted 350 sheep, ten cows, 40 goats, 30 pigs and 25 people (including 14 convicts). Ten years later, there were over 300 sheep and 1,000 cattle.

As the little town at Table Bay grew into the world-renowned 'Tavern of the Seas', the number of prisoners sent to the island slowly increased. Van Riebeeck's successor, Zacharias Wagenaar, declared that "the island makes a very good penitentiary where a rogue, after one or two years work in carrying shells, begins to sing very small." Nevertheless, several escape attempts were made over the years and, in 1673, five Khoikhoi convicts managed to steal a rudderless boat and successfully rowed themselves back to the mainland.

In the eighteenth century, the population of the island grew further with the arrival of prisoners from other parts of the Dutch East India Company's sphere of influence. Broadly referred to as *Indiaanen*, they included pirates, bandits and political leaders who had been banished from their homelands in the East for mounting insurrections against Dutch rule. Many of the political prisoners sent to the island during this time were of royal descent and several were also devout Muslims. The company hoped that incarceration on Robben Island would dampen their revolutionary fervour and reduce their popular support. Instead, the new arrivals succeeded in promoting Islam among the many Malay slaves resident at the Cape, thus adding to the Company's headaches. In 1722, of 42 prisoners resident on the island, 16 were *Indiaanen* and the rest were European.

One of the most famous of these political exiles was Sayed Adurohman Moturu, the Sheik of Madura, who had led a rebellion in Batavia (modern-day Indonesia). He died on Robben Island in 1754 and, even though his body was later taken back to Indonesia, the site of his grave was considered holy and became a place of pilgrimage for the Cape Muslim community. In 1969, a kramat (shrine) was built on the Sheik's burial site, right next to the maximum-security prison. Every February, a feast (the Khalifa) is held at the kramat. Another important religious figure to spend time on Robben Island is Tuan Guru, the first Chief Imam of the Cape Muslim community. He wrote a crucial text on Islam that became a standard reference work in the nineteenth century. He was imprisoned on the island from 1780 until his death in 1793.

OF VICTORIA

A yacht berthed at the Alfred
Basin, V&A Waterfront.

A colony of African pengiuns.

Above: Kramat shrine.
Centre strip: Soldier and General Infirmary graveyard.

Shipwrecks off the coast of Robben Island.

View of Table Mountain from Robben Island across endemic Cape fynbos.

Top: Blue slate quarry (northwestern side of the island).
Above: Van Riebeeck quarry (southern side of the island).

The lighthouse on Minto
Hill.

Facing: The lonely road
along the western shore.

Left: Razor wire and fences choke the maximum security prison.

Facing: Church of the Good Shepherd.

Below: Lonely sunlight in a cell.

Top: Governor's residence (now a guesthouse and conference centre).
Middle: Murray's Bay harbour.
Above: Communal cells.

Above: Bath of Bethesda.
Below and left: Leper
graveyard.

LEPER
GRAVEYARD

Above left: The derelict female asylum.
Above right: Disused prison football field.
Below: Abandoned house in the village.

Top: An old military gun emplacement.
Above: A disused military observation post.

Above: Jemiel plays on a naval gun at De Waal Battery.

Left: The old De Waal Battery.

Below: An old military observation post.

Conditions on the island during the 1700s are difficult to ascertain because of the lack of documentation and the absence of any extant buildings. One can only assume that life was no picnic. Most prisoners were forced to do hard labour on the island, quarrying stone or collecting shells. Food supplies were always low and rations were puny, prompting several protests by prisoners.

But any protests had to be discreet because, under Company rules, punishment for disobedience or insubordination was traditionally brutal. Beatings and lashes were commonplace. In one particularly unfortunate incident two men, Rijkhaart Jacobsz and a Khoikhoi prisoner called Claas Blank, were found guilty of sodomy. To teach them a lesson, they had weights tied to their bodies and were dumped into the sea. Many prisoners were also sentenced to live on the island 'in chains' and spent their days manacled to heavy iron links. There was even an attempt at a full-scale rebellion in 1751, but it was thwarted and the leaders were executed.

Yet none of this could stop the constant yearning for freedom and several escape attempts were made over the years. Indeed, many more people escaped from Robben Island than is generally acknowledged. Rowboats were occasionally stolen from the boathouse, and foreign ships would sometimes stop at the island illegally, hoping to pick up some additional crew members. Others may have even swum across the frigid channel to the mainland. The viability of surviving this crossing has been evidenced in the twentieth century by several long-distance swimmers, such as Peggy Duncan and Florrie Berndt who completed the marathon swim in the early 1920s without any kind of wetsuit or breathing apparatus. Still, for most people, the island was a fortress from which there was no escape.

The British, the Dutch and Napoleon's war

In 1795, there were about 90 prisoners on Robben Island.

By this time, the Dutch East India Company was nearly bankrupt and the days of Dutch rule at the Cape were numbered. This is because, back in Europe, Napoleon Bonaparte was embarking on his great imperial adventure and there were big upheavals across the continent.

At various times in the past, Britain and Holland had been sworn enemies as they competed over trade and territory. Faced with a common Napoleonic enemy, however, the two nations became allies. Therefore, when the French army invaded the Low Countries, the Duke of Orange, Holland's ruling monarch, was forced to flee for his life. King George III of England kindly offered sanctuary. Once safely ensconced in London, it was tactfully suggested to the Duke that Britain should take over Holland's foreign territories for safe keeping, especially that useful pitstop at the Cape of Good Hope, which was such an important part of the sea route to the East.

The Duke reluctantly agreed and Britain sent a fleet to take over and secure the Cape in 1795. Unfortunately, no one told the Dutch rulers in Cape Town and the British had to fight a short battle at Muizenberg before they could deliver the message. The first British occupation was thus a caretaking operation that lasted from 1795 to 1803. Then, a shaky peace with Napoleon was concluded and the Cape was given back to Holland, which was now re-invented as the French-controlled Republic of Batavia. This arrangement also didn't last long, however, and war soon flared up again, prompting the British to return to the Cape for a second occupation. This time, the British stayed for 100 years. They ruled the country as a colony from 1806 to 1910, expanding its territory into the interior and along the coast.

During this time, Robben Island once again proved itself to be a useful adjunct to the growing city of Cape Town. It was, of course, still utilized as a prison for criminal and political prisoners throughout the 1800s, but it was also used for a variety of additional enterprises. During the first half of the nineteenth century, for example, Robben Island was the site of a whaling station run by John Murray; a stone quarry run by Thomas Fitzpatrick; a quarantine station for infectious patients and a playground for upper-class types keen on a bit of hunting. In the second half of the century, a hospital of sorts was built, known as the General Infirmary, and a sad assortment of mental patients, lepers and paupers was sent there for 'recuperation' away from the genteel eyes of Cape society.

The co-existence of private enterprises and desperate prisoners was not always harmonious, however. John Murray's successful whaling station was forced to close down in 1820 after a group of prisoners stole some boats and escaped. Whales were, at that time, a common sight in the waters around the Cape Peninsula, until they were hunted out by the relentless Europeans. Fishermen, both legal and illegal, also proliferated in the waters around the island, occasionally tempting the various island overseers into private trade and profiteering—forbidden to civil servants.

As most of the Dutch-built buildings on the island were either destroyed or in ruins by the time the new British authorities took over, everything had to be built from scratch. Labour was supplied by prisoners, slaves, paid workers and sometimes even the soldiers, who were stationed on the island to keep an eye on the criminal element. Following the pattern of the Dutch, most of these new structures were erected on the southeastern part of the island, close to the harbour, and across from the huge bulk of Table Mountain looming over the channel.

Conditions on the island did improve somewhat after the British took over, especially in the 1820s and 1830s when the abolition of slavery and social reforms in England began to change the way that things were done. Humiliating public spectacles and physical punishments fell out of favour and incarceration became more humane. But, despite all the improvements and the commercial endeavours being run from the island, its fame (or notoriety) was still derived from its role as a feared prison for the state's enemies.

The Anglo-Xhosa wars

During the last decades of the Dutch regime and the first decades of British rule, the eastern frontier of the Cape had become troublesome and turbulent. The problem, as always, was land.

As European farmers migrated farther along the coast, they needed more and more land for their livestock. At first, the *trekboers* (literally meaning travelling farmers) found the land sparsely populated and the scattered locals easy to overcome. This was partly the result of a series of devastating smallpox epidemics that swept the entire region from 1717 onward, killing many Khoikhoi and shattering their clans and tribal groups. By the 1780s, however, the *trekboers* had reached the vicinity of the Great Fish River, near modern-day East London—and there they met the Xhosa.

The Xhosa were quite distinct from the Khoikhoi and Bushmen (San), who had hitherto been the only indigenous people to interact with the Europeans. Instead, this powerful nation was of Bantu lineage, having originated in West Africa before trekking down the African continent. This process started about 4,000 years ago. By 1000AD, Bantu-speaking migrants had settled along South Africa's eastern coast. They would eventually evolve into the Zulu and Xhosa cultural groups of today (the Nguni language grouping). Sotho-Tswana-speaking tribes, also of Bantu ancestry, arrived later and chose to settle on the high plateau of the interior.

The Europeans were totally unprepared to come face to face with this populous, powerful nation of tall, well-built warriors who were ready to fight for their fertile homelands. Similarly, the Xhosa were unprepared to deal with the tenacious long-hairs who wore strange clothes and carried fire-sticks. Tensions arose immediately.

It didn't help matters that the voracious European farmers who had taken land around the new settlement of Graaff-Reinet were a wild and lawless bunch. For several generations, they had lived away from the explicit control of the Cape and they were used to making their own rules. The Boers therefore saw no problem in sending raiding parties into Xhosa territory to steal cattle, while simultaneously demanding that the authorities at the Cape secure additional land for their enlarged herds. Xhosa chiefs soon retaliated and attacked Boer farms. Such temerity infuriated the Europeans even more. Additionally, the formerly passive Bushmen (or San) living in the Sneeuberg Mountains, near Graaff-Reinet, also decided that enough was enough and began sending raiding parties onto the Boer farms to steal or scatter their cattle. Then, some of the Khoikhoi (who were in the service of the Boers) rebelled and joined the side of the Xhosa to fight against the white interlopers.

To add to the general state of confusion, liberal missionaries began to make inroads among the Xhosa and started agitating against slavery and Boer aggression, much to the disgust of the white farmers. And, finally, the British, in their infinite wisdom, decided to initiate a policy of state-sponsored emigration from Britain to South Africa, and offered prospective settlers free farmland in the Grahamstown area—right bang in the middle of all the action. Garnish all this with some choice political mismanagement and poorly conceived government policy, and it's easy to see why things became such a mess.

Clearly, the whole area was a volatile powder keg, and the fuse had been lit. For nearly a century after the 1780s there would be little peace along the eastern frontier of the colony. Despite the attempts of Dutch (and later British) authorities to maintain control, a series of nine armed conflicts devastated this beautiful region and took a heavy toll on Europeans and local tribes alike. Even today, the Eastern Cape is a conflicted province, still living with the legacy of its difficult past. The people here continued to suffer greatly under apartheid and it remains one of the poorest areas in the country.

The details of these Anglo–Xhosa wars (also called the Xhosa Wars of Resistance or the Frontier Wars) are intricate and complicated, and it is beyond the scope of this book to discuss them at length. However, it is important to understand something about this period because many of the Xhosa leaders who were captured during the Frontier Wars were exiled to Robben Island and thus became the second generation of political prisoners to inhabit the island.

It is also worth noting that, in 1832, slavery was abolished within the British Empire. This caused a storm of consternation among the slave-owning farmers in the Eastern Cape. It was the last straw and many families packed up their things and embarked on a Great Trek away from Xhosa and the *donderse* English. These trekkers created two new Boer republics in the interior and, eventually, became the ideological fathers of apartheid. This necessitated the emergence of black political resistance in the twentieth century. It is always the case in history (as in life) that everything is connected.

The second generation

The first generation of political prisoners on Robben Island were Cape Khoikhoi, who opposed Dutch rule, and exiled rebel leaders from other parts of the Dutch East India Company's empire, such as Indonesia. The second generation, as has been discussed above, were indigenous leaders from the Eastern Cape frontier who were captured and sent to the island, sometimes accompanied by their wives and children.

It must have been a lonely existence for the Xhosa captives, stranded on a barren island, far away from the lush valleys and rushing rivers of their homeland. Many of them (particularly the women) became depressed and suicidal and longed to return to their families. They were not alone in their misery because, at this time, the island was also used to house criminal prisoners, military prisoners and some insane people who were thought to be a danger to society.

While it would be unfeasible to furnish a complete list of all the resistance leaders who spent time on the island during this period, it's worth mentioning a few of the better-known exiles. One of the first was Hans Trompetter, a Khoikhoi who had been sent to the island for his role in the Third Frontier War (1799–1803). He was later joined by David Stuurman, another Khoikhoi agitator, who was captured in 1809. Stuurman soon escaped from the island and returned to the frontier, where he was arrested a second time in 1819.

By this time, the ranks of banished Xhosa leaders had swelled to include Makhanda (also called Makanna, Nxele or Links—the latter meaning 'left-handed'). Makhanda was a powerful prophet who preached a strange combination of mysticism, Christianity (which he had learned from the missionaries) and Xhosa nationalism. In 1819, he led an ill-fated attack on Grahamstown and was defeated, thus ending the Fifth Frontier War. Upon his capture, he was sent to Robben Island, which became known to the Xhosa as Makhanda's Island.

In 1820, Trompetter, Stuurman and Makhanda were instrumental in organizing a mass escape from Robben Island. Exact numbers are unclear but a group of prisoners managed to overpower the guards and steal several longboats that belonged to John Murray's whaling station, which was operating from the harbour. Two of the boats capsized while crossing the rough sea, including the one carrying Makhanda. It is said that he clung to a rock, shouting encouragement to his fellow escapees, until waves pulled him down into the water. It is still unclear whether he drowned or survived, but his name does not appear in the records again. As a memorial to Makhanda, one of the tourist ferries to the island was named in his honour, but this vessel has now been decommissioned. The passengers of the one boat that did make it to shore faced a similarly dire fate. Only two people escaped subsequent capture and the others were convicted of 'mutiny and open violence with arms'. Trompetter and Johan Schmidt (one of the white organizers) were hanged and had their decapitated heads stuck on steel spikes as a warning to other prisoners. Several others were condemned to public flagellation with whips that had a piece of metal attached to the tip. The rest were sent back to Robben Island and forced to do hard labour. David Stuurman was saved from this fate because he had intervened to save the life of Murray's overseer, and was transported to Australia instead. He thus became the only person to successfully escape from Robben Island twice.

After a short lull in fighting on the frontier, the eighth and penultimate frontier war flared up between 1850 and 1853. The catalyst was a prophet called Mlanjeni who told the Xhosa that they could make themselves impervious to bullets. Sadly, this wasn't true and the war turned into another long and brutal affair. After an extensive campaign, the Xhosa were finally defeated and Siyolo, an important chief of the Ndlambe tribe, was captured and sent to Robben Island with his wife, for 17 years.

The other chiefs who fought in the war evaded the British for several more years but a great tragedy was about to unfold that would cripple the Xhosa nation and hasten its destruction at the hands of the British. This time, however, the danger came from within and it revolved around a young girl named Nongqawuse.

It all began in 1856, when Nongqawuse saw some strange apparitions rise up out of a river near her house. The human-like forms told her that the white man would be driven from the land by ancestral spirits, but only if the Xhosa people killed all their cattle and burned all their grain as a sign of faith. Unfortunately, Nongqawuse was the only one who could see or hear these phantom emissaries but her uncle, Mhalakaza, was also a spiritualist and believed her implicitly. He spread the message far and wide, canvassing the support of chiefs and common people alike.

Despite the severity of the prophesy, it spread like wildfire through the Xhosa nation, who were desperate to be rid of the violent and thieving white man. Furthermore, this wasn't the first time that a Xhosa seer had made such a prophesy. Makhanda and Mlanjeni both spoke along similar lines and Xhosa history is filled with stories of spiritual interventions by the ancestors. Although there were many who opposed this 'great cattle-killing', the believers eventually won out and most of the Xhosa people slaughtered all their cattle in anticipation of the day when the dead would arise, to drive out the settlers and resurrect the cattle.

Tragically, on the appointed day when the sun was supposed to rise red in the sky, nothing happened. The Xhosa people were left hopeless and hungry. Many thousands starved to death, including Mhalakaza and his family. Nongqawuse survived, under the protection of the British, and only died after 1905.

The British authorities were both horrified and delighted. The might of the Xhosa had been broken by their own hand and the resistance was effectively over. The British then capitalized on their gains by arresting as many chiefs as they could under the ridiculous pretext that the chiefs had planned the cattle-killing as a way to encourage their starving people to invade the colony. The colonial authorities also arrested a number of other Xhosa for stealing and, in 1857, as many as 900 prisoners were sent to Robben Island.

Among them were the great chiefs Mhala, Pato, Xoxo, Tola, Stokwe, Xayimpi, Maqoma, Maqoma's wife Kayti, and several other noble sons and daughters. The prisoners lived in traditional Xhosa huts built close to Murray's Bay and were supplied with meagre rations that they had to cook themselves. Even though they were not subjected to hard labour, their exile must have been devastating. Kayti, when she was ill, refused medicine saying, "No. My heart is sore. I want to die."

Gradually, the prisoners were released throughout the 1860s, and Maqoma, Xoxo and Siyolo were finally freed in 1869. All returned to their homelands in the Eastern Cape but their traditional territories had been annexed by the British and they found themselves effectively homeless. By this time, Maqoma was old and tired and he wanted to retire to a farm where he could live out his years in peace. So, he legally bought a piece of land near to his old stomping ground and moved there with his family. For no apparent reason he was removed by British troops. Indignant, Maqoma tried to return to his farm. This time, he was arrested and sent back to Robben Island. He died a lonely death on the island in 1873, at the age of 75.

In 1978, however, one of Maqoma's descendants was the Minister of the Interior for the then-independent 'homeland' of Transkei. He applied to the white government of the day for permission to retrieve the bones of his ancestor from Robben Island so that they could be brought back to the Eastern Cape for a proper burial. This request was, rather surprisingly, granted and a delegation arrived on the island with a traditional Xhosa diviner to find the bones of Maqoma. This was duly accomplished and the old chief was finally placed to rest in Hero's Acre, at the top of the Amatola Mountains.

Siyolo, for his part, was caught up in the Ninth Frontier War of 1877 and was killed in action. Sandile, the leader of the Ngqika chiefdom, was also killed during this last gasp of resistance. After the final conflict, several more Xhosa rebels were sent to the island, including the sons of Maqoma, Mhala and Sandile. The Xhosa were thus a nation defeated and their proud independence was broken, to be replaced with subordination to the British Empire.

It should be remembered, however, that the British were fighting the locals on all sides of their expanding South African territory. Accordingly, there were other political prisoners besides the Xhosa who spent time on Robben Island during the 1800s. Some Bushmen and Khoikhoi were sent there because of their role in the Bokkeveld Rebellion of 1824. The Zulu chief Langalibalele, head of the Hlubi tribe, was held there from 1874 to 1875 for his rebellion against the British forces in Natal. And the leaders of the Koranna Wars, fought along the Orange River in 1870 and 1879, were also imprisoned for their refusal to honour Queen and Country.

The barren, tiny island must have been a terrible place for these proud and once-powerful men, so far removed from all that they had known and loved. Contemporary photographs of the prisoners taken on the island show us faces which are lined with sadness and despair. It must have been a bitter time. Nevertheless, it does show us that the island has long been associated with native resistance against an unjust system of government. It also demonstrates that the list of South African martyrs stretches back to well before the curse of apartheid in the twentieth century.

Lepers and lunatics

By the mid-1800s, attitudes to imprisonment had changed. Incarceration for life was seen as a waste of resources and the notion that prisoners could be reformed and re-integrated into society had been mooted. The new British governor at the Cape, John Montagu, was a firm believer in this approach, especially since the colony needed cheap labour to complete the ambitious programme of public works that he had proposed.

So, from the 1840s onward, many of the criminal prisoners on Robben Island were transferred to the mainland where they could work off their debt to society in a more constructive manner. For the rest of the century, convicted criminals would be used to construct roads, dams, bridges, harbours and all the other modern conveniences of a British colony. Specifically, convict labour gangs were extensively used to improve and construct the treacherous mountain passes that had hitherto limited British exploitation of the interior. Many of our most spectacular passes, including the Swartberg Pass and Sir Lowry's Pass, were therefore built by convicts (who were usually housed in well-guarded compounds, built at strategic points along the proposed route). Some of these structures still remain as ruined reminders of the blood, sweat and tears that went into the construction of the roads we drive today.

But Montagu did not stop there. He was a progressive leader and believed that the resources of Robben Island should not be wasted. He therefore re-invented Robben Island as a place of recuperation and restoration. After all, the fresh sea breeze and bracing climate of the island were said to be good for body and soul.

It also happened that the island was an ideal place to send the mentally disturbed, chronically poor and incurably sick; people who would otherwise have depressed the healthy citizens of South Africa. Sticking these unfortunate souls on the island, far away from the eyes and conscience of the populace, seemed to be an ideal solution and, from 1846 to 1931, Robben Island was predominantly used as an isolation tank for the socially undesirable.

Following Montagu's exhortation that 'the salubrity of Robben Island has long been acknowledged, and there is an abundance of stone, lime and labour on the spot to erect the necessary buildings', the lepers from the Hemel-en-Aarde settlement near Caledon and the Baakens River settlement near Port Elizabeth were moved to Robben Island in 1845. In the following year, over 100 paupers and chronically sick patients from various asylums around the Cape colony were also sent to island, along with 50 lunatics from the Somerset Hospital in Cape Town. The remaining prisoners on the island were tasked with turning a jail into a hospital and, over the years, a number of buildings were erected to house and care for the new inhabitants. This collection of structures came to be known as the General Infirmary.

However, despite the governor's best intentions, many of the new arrivals did not relish the thought of being sent to Robben Island. It was still a desolate place, associated with exile and desperation, and it was far removed from any family and social support which may have sustained them. The different groups now resident on the island also had very little in common. The lunatics were often delusional, disruptive and violent. The lepers were reviled because of their disease (which was poorly understood) and resented their involuntary exile. The poor and chronically sick had similar concerns about being packed off to the island. And the remaining prisoners, who were seen as dangerous, or beyond reform, were a thorn in the side of everyone. It should also be mentioned that the General Infirmary contained both male and female patients from all racial groups and social classes.

At the time, however, the state did not overly concern itself with any of this and left the responsibility for caring for the sick and indigent to missionaries and church groups. Although there was a corps of British staff stationed on the island, most of the custodians of the General Infirmary were priests and nuns who did their best to cater for the needs of their charges in very trying circumstances. Initially, the old governor's residence was converted into the 'female residence' for the chronically sick, the lepers were housed in the stables, and the lunatics roamed around the old prison (parts of which still stand today, abandoned and forlorn). Chronically sick male patients were housed in a number of buildings, most of which were entirely unsuitable for the purpose.

Many of these missionaries were Irish, and the little village that grew up on the southeastern part of the island became known as Irish Town. The island's Anglican church, which had been built in 1841, was therefore a focal point of community life. However, fears of contamination by the lepers resulted in the construction of a second church,

EARLY HISTORY

the Church of the Good Shepherd, in 1895. This humble structure was designed by Sir Herbert Baker and contained no pews, as lepers were deemed to be only comfortable when lying down or standing up. When the island's next occupants, the military, arrived in the 1930s, they wanted to tear down the church because they feared the disease was still lurking in the stone walls, but church authorities forbade them and the refuge of the Good Shepherd still stands on the outskirts of today's village.

The lepers, who were mostly black and poor, were a particularly unfortunate group. Firstly, they were victims of a horrible disease (which then had no known cure) and, secondly, they were victims of an ignorant and unforgiving society which shunned them as unclean and hazardous.

Even today, common misconceptions about leprosy suggest a virulent and highly contagious disease that makes your fingers fall off and your skin rot. The reality, however, is far less fearsome.

Also known as Hansen's disease, leprosy is caused by a parasitic bacterium called *Mycobacterium leprae*. It reproduces very slowly, causing considerable damage to the skin, mucous membranes and nerves if left untreated. It does not, however, make the skin rot. Instead, it causes inflammation, lesions and thickening of the skin. It can also cause damage to the nerves, causing a loss of feeling that leads to inadvertent injury and infection.

Today, leprosy is easily treated with multi-drug antibiotics but, historically, it was incurable and greatly feared. The lowly status of lepers as 'unclean' or 'cursed' seems to have its roots in antiquity, featuring quite prominently in the bible, and the disease was long thought to be highly infectious. The truth, however, is that 95% of the world's population is naturally immune to leprosy and the disease is only active (i.e. infectious) for a short period. It remains a mysterious malady, however, and the precise mode of transmission is still unknown (although it is thought to be spread through respiratory droplets, like its bacterial cousin, tuberculosis).

Currently, there are about one to two million people around the world living with leprosy, with 760,000 new cases being reported in 2002. While India, Mozambique, Myanmar (Burma), Madagascar, Tanzania and Nepal contain 90% of the modern world's leprosy patients, even first-world countries are not immune. America reported just over 100 cases of the disease in 1999. Despite modern medical treatment and research, several countries around the world still maintain leper asylums, where sufferers are kept in quarantine even though there is no scientific evidence that this precaution is necessary.

On Robben Island, the custodians of the General Infirmary cared for the lepers as best they could. In addition to giving them powerful and unnecessary purgatives, it was thought that sea water was beneficial for those living with the disease, and a tidal pool was constructed at the far-end of the island where they could bathe. The remains of this pool, called the Bath of Bethesda, are still visible today and the stagnant, black water that lies within the crumbling stone retaining wall is an evocative echo of an unhappy community.

When I visited the bath, I sat on the seaward wall and contemplated the murky depths of the pool. After a few moments of reverie, however, I found myself struck by a sudden and irrational fear that some rogue bacteria may have survived the intervening 70 years and was about to infect me with this ancient disease. Despite my modern education and liberal outlook, the power and stigma of leprosy was still so strong that I walked away from the pools a little bit faster than was necessary.

The lepers of the Cape were thus torn away from any family and friends that they might have had and dumped on the island. The mentally disturbed were similarly misunderstood and ill-treated by contemporary society. Although it was mainly the dangerous or violent lunatics who were shipped off to Robben Island, there are many touching stories of harmless old nutcases who were forced to live out their days on the lonely rock, with only the distant view of Table Mountain for company.

One such character is Plaatjies, a coloured man, who spent his days combing the shore for bits of wood from which he planned to build a boat that would take him back to the mainland. Each time he managed to cobble together a little vessel, however, the authorities would find the craft and destroy it, forcing Plaatjies to start all over again. This modern-day Sisyphus was so convinced that he would one day return to civilization, he even created and inscribed his own coins that he planned to use in the shops of Cape Town.

The paupers and chronically sick also didn't have an easy time of it. While several formerly well-to-do citizens of Cape Town actually requested a place on Robben Island so that their neighbours wouldn't see how they had fallen on hard times, most of the indigent people were unwilling inmates of the General Infirmary. Some of them were destitute ex-slaves, others were too ill to support themselves on the mainland. All were unhappy and miserable. While the poor and sick were usually supplied with food from the government, the rations were miserly and the patients were often made to do hard labour in the quarries and at the harbour to earn their keep.

As in the past, living conditions on the island were dire. The water supply was brackish, the climate was unforgiving, the loneliness was overwhelming and diseases such as dysentery were prevalent. The island staff were not much better off, living in damp homes and earning a very low wage. Furthermore, the resident Surgeon-Superintendent had tremendous power over the island and standards of living varied considerably depending upon who was in charge. Indeed, many of the people who held power tended to become cruel and bitter as a result of being cooped up on the island, far away from the humanizing influence of society and the beady eyes of the colonial authorities. This is the dark side of living in such an insular community. It has always been a factor of life on Robben Island, especially in the twentieth century when prison guards would egg each other on to treat the prisoners with ever-increasing levels of brutality.

In the 1850s, however, a number of scandals broke regarding conditions on the island and the authorities were forced to dismiss the superintendent. In the 1860s, a new superintendent tried to reform the treatment of lunatics, replacing chains and beatings with occupational therapy and humane supervision. But facilities were still woefully inadequate and the status of the inmates did not really justify the cost of building new structures. The first major renovations of the General Infirmary were only undertaken in the 1890s.

Nevertheless, thanks to the reforms on the island, the mental institution began to attract larger numbers of middle-class, white patients whose families were prepared to pay for their treatment. This swelled the number of people living on Robben Island. Then, in 1891, a worldwide leprosy scare caused the government to pass the Leprosy Repression Act, which made it compulsory for all lepers (who were mostly black) to be kept in a suitable asylum. This caused another influx of people to arrive in Murray's Bay. Ironically, before the 1891 Act, all the lepers were technically free to leave the island whenever they wanted to, but the sneaky colonial authority kept this useful fact from the unfortunate pariahs.

As a result of all this, by 1892, there were 1,070 people living on the island. By 1896, the island had its own primary school, a guesthouse, the above-mentioned Church of the Good Shepherd and a new pier—all of which are still standing today.

The increased numbers of lepers on the island now gave them enough clout to mount several protests about their 'imprisonment' and poor quality of life. In 1892, the male lepers demanded to be allowed access to the female lepers and, in 1893, the female lepers initiated a strike and refused to do any work, demanding to be treated like patients and not like prisoners. In both cases, additional troops were sent in as 'leper police' and the revolts were put down.

For the next few decades, the debate about lepers raged. Doctors argued about whether or not they were a danger to society. Some shipping companies refused to transport lepers as passengers. Several families hid their leprous relatives to prevent their incarceration. Meanwhile, on Robben Island, the increasing numbers of white lepers resulted in systematic segregation of the inmates for the first time (although various forms of racial discrimination had been unofficially practised since the 1850s). It was even stated that patients should first be divided according to race and then, if possible, according to the progression of their disease!

As was often the case in the past (and as would be the case in the future), rations, clothing and privileges were all allocated according to the colour of one's skin. Rich white patients were even allowed to pay for their own rooms and several free-standing cottages were built so that they wouldn't have to mix with the undesirable black and coloured lepers. After protests from the coloured lepers in 1904, some of these discriminatory practices were toned down, but the end result was that the privileges of the paying patients were simply extended to all the white patients, regardless of their financial standing.

But the days of the General Infirmary were coming to an end. Running a medical institution, even a rudimentary one, on Robben Island was becoming increasingly expensive and controversial. By 1921, all the lunatics had been moved from the island to Valkenberg Asylum on the mainland, where they were required to undertake 'institutional labour' as part of their treatment. The chronically sick were similarly relocated to the mainland from the 1890s onward.

Then, in 1931, the League of Nations Health Organization stated that compulsory segregation of lepers was no longer necessary and should be replaced with a more lenient 'isolation' policy that made allowance for infectious and non-infectious cases of the disease. Since the incidence of leprosy had been in a steady decline for the previous few decades, public hysteria about the disease had abated and the leper asylum on Robben Island was closed that same year. The remaining patients were sent to Westfort Hospital near Pretoria.

Robben Island was now largely abandoned, and it remained more or less empty for five years. It would be nice to think of this as a time when the island could take a deep breath and recuperate from four centuries of human depredation, violence and misery. The respite was brief, however, and when Robben Island was re-inhabited in 1936, it became the home of a very different kind of inmate.

The military years

It is somewhat ironic that one of the happiest times on Robben Island was when it was used for war. It could even be said that, apart from its current incarnation as a museum, the years from 1936 to 1960 were the proudest in the island's long and mostly tragic history. These were the military years, when army and naval troops lived on the island and protected the mainland from an anticipated invasion by the Germans.

But initially, after the leper asylum was finally closed down in 1931, the fate of the island was uncertain. By this time, there were 170 buildings on the island, in various states of repair. Ninety of these were promptly destroyed because they had been 'contaminated' by the lepers, and the others were left to decay in quiet abandonment.

During this time, several plans for the island were mooted. It was going to be a vegetable garden, a hunting ground, a hotel and a sanatorium, but nothing came of these suggestions. In the meantime, people began to visit the silent island for recreation and fishing. Camping trips became quite popular and a group of Girl Guides even had to be rescued when they found themselves stranded there.

In 1933, however, Adolf Hitler rose to power in Germany and plunged the world into a global struggle, which would culminate in the dreadful waste of human life that came to be called World War II. Back in South Africa allegiances were divided. The English-speakers were clearly on the side of Britain and the allied powers. The Afrikaners, for their part, generally favoured the German cause or advocated a neutral stance in the European conflict. This caused a rift in the coalition government between J. B. Herzog's Nationalist Party and Jan Smuts' South African Party. At this time, the Minister of Defence was a staunch Nationalist named Oswald Pirow and he used the tensions brewing in the northern hemisphere as a good excuse to shore up South Africa's military defences. Whether this decision was in anticipation of a German attack or in preparation for a civil war is difficult to determine.

In any event, Pirow noted that Robben Island's strategic position at the entrance to Table Bay made it the ideal location for a new military base and declared the entire island to be military property. A gun battery was subsequently transferred from Signal Hill to Robben Island, largely because the concussion caused by the firing of these guns on the mainland tended to shatter windows in Green Point. Additional plans were also drawn up to strengthen the island's defences.

War officially broke out in 1939, and Italy and Japan joined the fray in 1940 and 1941 respectively. The ensuing conflict made the Mediterranean and Suez Canal dangerous for allied shipping and the old sea route around the Cape re-assumed its previous importance. With Japanese ships prowling the Indian Ocean and the unseen threat of German U-boats menacing the Atlantic, it became imperative that the safety of Cape Town be upheld.

Tensions continued to grow within the government and Herzog eventually resigned as Prime Minister, leaving the pro-British Smuts in charge. Accordingly, the Department of Public Works was ordered to fortify the island. 150,000 tons of building material was laboriously shipped across the sea, and teams of labourers were soon building roads, barracks, a landing strip, observation towers, outlooks, rifle posts, troop compounds and the other paraphernalia of battle. Most of the older buildings were demolished and the rubble was used to build a new harbour at Murray's Bay. Finally, a desalinization plant was constructed to supplement the island's traditionally poor water supply.

The two gun batteries were constructed: the Cornelia Battery overlooked the Blouberg channel and the De Waal Battery protected the entrance to Table Bay. They eventually boasted an assortment 6-inch- and 9.2-inch-calibre guns. During the war, four 3.7-inch and two 40mm Bofors guns were added to the arsenal, along with a dummy battery that was to act as a decoy. Along with the batteries at Simon's Town and Llandudno, it was hoped that these coastal defences would stave off any hostile invaders. A complex degaussing circuit was also constructed to protect passing ships from the magnetic mines that were being used by the Germans, and cables were laid along the ocean floor to detect pesky U-boats.

Despite all this planning, there was never an actual attack on Cape Town and the guns were never fired in battle. They were fired for tests and drills, however, and on one occasion, they set the surrounding gum trees alight and caused a terrific bonfire. But this is not to say that South Africa was free from threat. German U-boats did prowl the waters off the Cape and harried several allied fleets as they sailed up the West Coast. There are even reports of one U-boat (U-172) sneaking into the mouth of Table Bay for a look-see. Other U-boats are reported to have been active along the Natal coast, where they may have met up with local Nazi sympathizers, such as the *Ossewa Brandwag* organization.

Thus, during the war years and beyond, thousands of troops made their home on Robben Island. Gunners, engineers, medics, chaplains, infantry and naval troops from both the British and South African forces all served on Robben Island, either on active duty or in training. Additionally, coloured soldiers from the re-formed Cape Corps and female soldiers from the Women's Auxiliary Army Service (WAAS), Women's Auxiliary Air Force (WAAF) and the South African Women's Auxiliary Naval Service (SWANS) were also used to bolster the country's war effort when the supply of white men ran low. Obviously, these 'lesser' recruits were treated as auxiliary troops with lower pay and prestige.

Nevertheless, the female presence on the island was considerable and the SWANS, WAASs and WAAFs all went to work (often to the consternation of their male superiors). While most of them were assigned clerical duties, many women also trained as range-takers, radar operators and signal controllers, acquitting themselves admirably in these tasks. The female contingent also contributed to raising morale on the island by organizing dances, planting flowers, having picnics and just by being so dashed lovely.

With all these men and women sharing such a small space, it seems obvious that love would occasionally blossom among the leaky tents. We know, for example, of at least one young SWAN, named Bridget, who met the man of her dreams while on active duty. He was a young soldier named Harry Oppenheimer and they went on to have a long and wealthy marriage.

Once the war ended in 1945, most of the troops were withdrawn from Robben Island. The military, however, still held onto the strategically important outpost until 1960 and used the infrastructure they had built as a coastal artillery school. The many barracks, outlooks, rifle posts and observation towers slowly fell into disuse but a small community of semi-permanent residents took over the old 'Irish Town' and made the village their own. Several people have subsequently written of an idyllic childhood spent on Robben Island—safe yet isolated—where the only action was the occasional military manoeuvre and the booming of the battery guns, sometimes fired as part of a drill.

But, once again, things were about to change. In 1948, the National Party won the (white) general election and Smuts was removed from power. It was the start of 50 years of oppression and hatred—an era that has come to be summarized by the word 'apartheid'.

Over the next few decades, the government would gradually implement a series of laws that were designed to curtail the liberties of black and coloured South Africans. While the motivations for this debilitating raft of legislation were undoubtedly based on the prejudice inherited from their Boer ancestors, do not assume that apartheid was only about racial ideology. There was another overriding reason for this calculated policy of denigration—the need to ensure that the pure-white state always had a steady supply of cheap black labour.

Obviously, this approach to government was going to cause resistance and protest in a country with an overwhelming black majority. The authorities therefore realized that they would need a place to incarcerate all the troublemakers. Thus, in 1959, the Minister of Justice announced that Robben Island was going to become a prison once again. The military installations were relocated to the mainland and all access to the island was restricted. A new and terrible chapter in the island's history had begun.

Today, the vestiges of its military years are all over the island—the coastline is dotted with lookout-posts, observation towers peep over the trees and ruined barracks cover the open field next to Van Riebeeck's old quarry. The guns of the Cornelia Battery have been removed, but the camouflaged concrete emplacements remain, hidden in the trees. The enormous guns of the De Waal Battery are still intact but slowly rusting away in the salty air, ever vigilant against an attack by a phantom Luftwaffe.

Even more eerie are the kilometres of underground tunnels and control rooms that were presumably to be used in the event of an air raid. I was first told of these tunnels by a local kid, Jemiel, who plays around the old guns with his friends. I was intrigued and he kindly offered to take me through the tunnels after school on the following day. When we arrived at the De Waal Battery, we climbed down a steep flight of stairs and entered a low concrete tunnel. It soon became so dark I couldn't tell if my eyes were open or closed. At first, I tried to appear nonchalant about the whole experience but I quickly lost my composure as the tunnel twisted and turned in the inky blackness. Luckily, the fearless nine-year-old took me by the hand and led me through the spooky labyrinth until we reached the blessed sunlight. I'm glad I wasn't a soldier in World War II. I'm too much of a *wuss*.

The apartheid years

And so, after nearly 500 turbulent years, we come to what, for many, is the main attraction—Robben Island as the prison that held Mandela and the other resistance leaders who opposed apartheid.

This chapter covers a particularly traumatic time on an island that had already been forced to witness many unspeakable tragedies. As such, it has proven to be a daunting and difficult section to write. Perhaps it's because the scar is still recent, too fresh in the memory to be dulled by the soothing distance of history. Or perhaps it is a result of the deference and respect I feel for the people involved— the named and the nameless, the living and the dead—who sacrificed so much for our current liberty. But it is a story that all South Africans, and citizens of the world, need to know ... and at least it has a happy ending.

We'll start with the British.

Since they took over the Cape from the Dutch in 1806, the British had presided over a tumultuous colony that never ceased to surprise them. First it was the Xhosa wars (as recounted above). Then it was the Voortrekkers, heading off into the interior to make their own country where they could raise their slaves in peace, away from *rooinek* interference. Then it was the whole Anglo–Zulu War business in Natal. And then diamonds in Kimberley. And then gold on the Witwatersrand. By the end of the century, the frazzled colonial authorities back in London were at their wits end.

The only thing for it was to take over the whole country and put the place to order—only problem was the Boers. They had set up two ramshackle republics in the north—the Orange Free State and the Zuid-Afrikaanse Republic, or Transvaal—and they wouldn't give them up without a fight.

This fight finally took place between 1899 and 1902. It was called the Second Anglo–Boer War (also known as the South African War) and it was a bitter, drawn-out affair. The end result, by attrition, was the surrender of the Boers. This was followed by years of negotiation as to how to rule the land. Finally, in 1910, the Union of South Africa was inaugurated as a self-governing state under the crown, with a whites-only franchise that excluded all people of colour from the vote. In terms of franchise, non-whites were worse off than before the war. This harsh dispensation was granted with the blessing of the British government, despite an impassioned plea from a group called the South African Native Congress who first met at Queenstown in 1907.

The first major act of the Union Government, under Louis Botha, was the Land Act of 1913. It was a hideous piece of legislation that effectively declared over 90% of the country as 'white areas' in which people of colour were not allowed to own land. The blacks were to be relocated to 'native reserves' where they could enjoy a modicum of self-determination and would only be allowed into the 'white areas' for the purpose of providing labour. Although the full stipulations of the Land Act would not be enforced for several decades, this ludicrous plan was to be the blueprint for the next fifty years of government policy.

The black people could clearly see which way the wind was blowing and it was partly in anticipation of this Land Act that the African National Congress was formally established in 1912. The first figurehead of the movement was Pixley Ka Isaka Seme, who requested "all the dark races of this subcontinent to come together, once or twice a year, in order to review the past and reject therein all those things which have retarded our progress."

After the Second World War, the relatively liberal South African Party of Jan Smuts was defeated by the Boer-dominated National Party, under D. F. Malan, in the general election of 1948. Over the next decade, a series of laws was passed that diminished and humiliated the black people of South Africa. There was the Urban Areas Act, the Mixed Marriages Act, the Population Registration Act ... and worse was yet to come.

In 1958, a grand visionary took over as Prime Minister, Dr. H. F. Verwoerd. With his honeyed words, this vicious visionary painted a poisonous picture of 'apartheid' and separate development where the black people would be turned into the 'hewers of wood and the drawers of water'. In exchange for their labour and subservience, Verwoerd promised to look after the blacks in the best tradition of Christian guardianship. After all, whitey knows best.

Despite his constant half-smile, Verwoerd knew full well that there would be opposition from the African people. The decision was taken to prepare Robben Island as a prison for all of those who opposed the state. The 'Treason Trial', in which 150 defendants of all races were charged with conspiracy, was already underway and, from 1961, criminal prisoners were sent to the island to help prepare the way for the anticipated influx of political prisoners. The Treason Trial, by the way, ended after four years with no convictions.

By this time, the ANC was a nationally supported organization and the movement had already led many, largely peaceful, protests against the government. Their lack of progress frustrated some, however, and one firebrand named Robert Sobukwe broke away from the ANC to start a more militant group, the Pan-Africanist Congress (PAC), in 1959.

In 1960, the mass-action Defiance Campaign was mounted against the draconian Pass Laws that restricted the movement of black people through 'white areas'. At one of these protests, outside a police station in Sharpeville, near Vereeniging, the police opened fire on the crowd. 69 people were killed, most of whom were shot in the back as they fled. The event shocked the nation and the international community. The South African government's reaction was swift. The ANC and the PAC were declared illegal organizations and banned. New laws were promulgated to make it easier to arrest and imprison opposition leaders. In 1961, Verwoerd left the British Commonwealth and declared South Africa a republic. For their part, both the PAC and the ANC decided to take up arms in the struggle against apartheid, and both established military wings, named *Poqo* ('The real owners [of Africa]') and *Umkhonto we Siswe* ('Spear of the nation'), respectively. It was war.

In the aftermath of Sharpeville, the first political prisoners to be arrested and sent to Robben Island were mainly PAC and Poqo members. They arrived from 1961 onward, landing on a rough island, only recently abandoned by the military. It was in no way ready to be maximum-security prison. The first prisoners were therefore quickly put to work quarrying stone and building their cells.

They were soon joined by representatives of the other opposition groups, who were systematically rounded up and packed off to the island where they couldn't cause trouble. Over the years, members of the PAC, ANC, the South West Africa People's Organization (SWAPO), the National Liberation Front, the African People's Democratic Union of South Africa, the non-European Unity Movement, the Liberal Party, the United Democratic Front, the Indian Congress, the Azanian People's Organization (AZAPO), Black Consciousness leaders and many others would be incarcerated on Robben Island. The prison population was therefore far from homogenous and conflicts between the various factions did flare up from time to time.

Nevertheless, the prisoners soon began to collaborate with one another and presented a united face against the common enemy. Several veterans have described the camaraderie and friendship that existed between the prisoners as one of the few positive aspects of their life in jail.

Another unifying factor was that all these prisoners were black or of colour. But it should not be assumed that there were no white people in the resistance. Many white men and women were involved at all levels of the struggle but Robben Island was for non-white prisoners only. The whiteys were usually sent to Pretoria Central.

In 1962, the apartheid authorities caught themselves a big fish, a senior ANC official named Nelson Rolihlahla Mandela. He was captured while driving to Howick in Natal to meet with the ANC president, Albert Luthuli (South Africa's first Nobel Peace Prize winner). A wanted man, Mandela was disguised as a chauffeur, but the police had been tipped off (perhaps by the CIA) and he was arrested in the Natal Midlands.

Shortly afterwards, the police stumbled on a group of ANC bigwigs who were meeting at a farm called Liliesleaf in Rivonia, Johannesburg. They were all arrested and, along with Mandela, charged with treason, sabotage, communism and plotting to overthrow the government. The prosecution asked for the death penalty but, fearful of an international outcry, the 'Rivonia Eight' were sentenced to life imprisonment. Nelson Mandela, Walter Sisulu, Ahmed Kathrada, Andrew Mlangeni, Elias Motsoaledi, Govan Mbeki and Raymond Mhlaba were shipped off to Robben Island. Denis Goldberg was sent to Pretoria Central. With Luthuli under house arrest and Oliver Tambo in exile, the government had effectively silenced the opposition within a few short years. Nevertheless, the struggle would live on … underground.

At this point, it should again be mentioned that Robben Island was not the exclusive preserve of the ANC. It is tempting to be overwhelmed by the legitimate star power of Nelson Mandela and the Rivonia trialists but they are just one part of the story.

Thousands of 'ordinary' foot-soldiers were imprisoned on the island, along with other big names, such as John Nyathi Pokela, Johnson Mlambo, Zephania Mothopeng, Andimba Toivo ya Toivo (from SWAPO), Neville Alexander, Billy Nair, Sonny Venkatrathnam, Kader Hassim, Fikile Bam, Eddie Daniels, Mac Maharaj, Harry Gwala and Wilton Mkwayi (who fought the prison authorities for 25 years for permission to marry his beloved Irene). In the '70s and '80s, future political leaders such as Kgalema Motlanthe, Joe Seremane, Steve Tshwete, Tokyo Sexwale, Jacob Zuma, Saths Cooper, Mosiuoa 'Terror' Lekota, Strini Moodley and Ronnie Mamoepa also spent their time on the island.

In particular, one must also mention Robert Sobukwe, the founder of the PAC. Charismatic and defiant, Sobukwe was among the first political prisoners arrested in the chaotic days after Sharpeville. He was quickly convicted and spent three years in Pretoria Central. When his sentence was up, however, the government didn't want to release him as he was considered too dangerous. So, a new law was passed which stated that Sobukwe could be kept in custody indefinitely, without any further charges being levelled against him, until he could convince the authorities that would no longer agitate against the apartheid regime. It was called the 'Robert Sobukwe clause'.

Sobukwe refused absolutely to kowtow to the government's blackmail and was sent to Robben Island. But even here he was considered such a threat that he was not allowed to live in the main prison. Instead, he was put in a house on the outskirts of the village and kept apart from all the other prisoners. For nine years he lived in the tiny, two-roomed house under constant guard. He was not allowed visitors and was forbidden to speak to anyone. His isolation was so complete it is said that he partially lost the ability to speak. Periodically, a government stooge would arrive at the house and offer Sobukwe his freedom on condition he gave up the struggle. Sobukwe refused every time.

In 1969, Sobukwe was diagnosed with lung cancer and he was relocated to Kimberley where he lived for another nine years under constant house arrest. He died in 1978 and was buried in his hometown of Graaff-Reinet, where there is now a small Sobukwe museum. His house still stands on Robben Island, a bleak reminder of how far the apartheid government would go to silence its critics.

Even though Sobukwe's case was exceptional, treatment of all political prisoners on Robben Island was brutal and stupid, especially in the early years before 1965. Many of the warders were poorly educated and resented the erudition of some of their wards. The island was also far away from the eyes of the world and prison staff could get away with just about anything. Besides, it was exactly what terrorists, communists and enemies of the state deserved. To be fair, however, it should be mentioned that the life of a prison guard on Robben Island was tough. They had long shifts, thin uniforms and bullying superiors who spread hate and fear throughout the white community in the village.

This didn't make life easy for the political prisoners. Daily beatings, hard labour, paltry rations and harassment by the criminal prisoners who shared their cells was the norm. Prison warders, often led by vicious ringleaders such as the despised Kleynhans brothers, inflicted a stream of verbal and physical abuse on the politicos. This was exacerbated by the gangs of criminal prisoners who were chosen, says Moses Dlamini, "to come and demoralize and humiliate us with the assistance of the uncouth, uncivilized, raw boer warders so that we would never again dare to challenge the system of apartheid colonialism." As it turns out, the criminal prisoners were eventually moved to another facility on the island because the political prisoners were seen to be a bad influence on the gangsters.

Prison life and prisoner resistance

The prison was divided into two main sections—the single cells and the communal cells. The perceived leaders were kept in the single cells where they could not 'infect' the others, and the rank and file were kept in overcrowded communal cells. Despite this precaution, smuggled communications between the prisoners and their leadership were frequent and well co-ordinated, often with the assistance of the kitchen staff. The entire prison was soon organized into an effective system of political cells and hierarchies.

Education and the development of literacy skills was also a priority and there were many illicit documents about the history and future of the struggle circulating within the prison. Walter Sisulu and Govan Mbeki, father of Thabo, were both respected historians and played a large role in these discussions.

The prisoners were also divided into several groups, according to their racial classification: Indian, coloured or black. Each group had its own dietary regime, precisely measured out in ounces and spoonfuls, thought to best suit its temperament. The black prisoners had it the worst. They were not given bread and only received maize meal, as it was assumed to be their staple diet. They were also given the least amount of meat or fish (five ounces, four times a week). But all of this was moot because warders had carte blanche to withhold anyone's ration for up to three meals in succession as an arbitrary punishment for insubordination.

In terms of uniforms, black prisoners had to wear short pants and sandals with no socks, no matter what the weather. Indian and coloured prisoners could wear long pants and socks. All prisoners wore short-sleeved shirts—winter on the island must have chilled them to the bone. Bedding for all prisoners consisted of sisal mats and two blankets, which were laid out on the concrete floors. Beds were only introduced in the mid-1970s.

The prisoners were divided yet again into categories that dictated to what privileges they were entitled. Group A prisoners, considered the least dangerous, were allowed one visit and three letters a month. Group D prisoners, including Mandela, were allowed one visit and one letter every six months. Even then, this trickle of communication from the outside world was heavily censored by the prison warders. Prisoners were not allowed access to any news media whatsoever.

Most of the political prisoners were put to work in the quarries on the island and stories of how the warders beat and taunted the prisoners are simply appalling. Johnson Mlambo of the PAC was the victim of one particularly barbaric incident where he was buried up to his neck in sand so that the pathetic guards could urinate on his head. Ironically, the criminal prisoners were given the less strenuous jobs on the island and many were even allowed to work in the warders' homes.

One upside to the hard labour was that many of the most important leaders were assigned to the lime quarry, where they spent almost 13 years hacking away at the bright, white stone. Always quick to exploit an opening, the prisoners used this opportunity to consult with each other and discuss

Top: Maximum security prison.
Middle: Courtyard for solitary-cell prisoners.
Above: Communal cells.

Limestone quarry, the 'classroom' and tourist bus tour.

Above left: Guard tower
Above right: Towering prison walls.
Below: Nelson Mandela's cell.

Robert Sobukwe House.

Above left: The Nelson Mandela Gateway at the V&A Waterfront.
Above right: The Clock Tower at the V&A Waterfront.
Below: Gateway exhibition.

Above: Murray's Bay harbour.
Right: Boarding the tour bus.
Below: Main entrance to Robben Island.
Facing: The ferry approaches the island.

Passageway to an old
courtyard.

Above left: A simple reminder of
Bergselaar's drowning.
Above right: African penguin crossing.
Below: Faure pier.

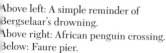

Robben Island
MUSEUM

NO ENTRY

GEEN TOEGANG

AKUNGENWA

African sacred ibis.

Top: Bontebok.
Above: Cape Town from the southern side of the island.

Village life on Robben Island.

Sport and recreation facilities in Robben Island village.

Top: The school.
Above: Primary school children at break.

their plans to improve conditions in the prison and beyond. When you visit the quarry today, you will see a small 'cave' cut into the rock face. This hole was used as a place where the prisoners could eat their lunch and sneak a hurried conversation away from the constant gaze of the warders. In order to further guarantee their privacy, the prisoners also used this hole as a toilet and the unpleasant smell kept the guards away.

Several veterans of the island have subsequently referred to the island as a 'university' and identified this hidey-hole as 'the classroom'. It is certainly true to say that the prisoners used their time in prison to refine their organizational structures, and the first non-racial government of South Africa was forged in the noisome confines of this cove. Hard labour in the quarry was finally suspended in 1977. Incidentally, the fine limestone dust and glaring reflection off the quarry walls affected the eyesight of several prisoners and, after his release, Nelson Mandela had to have a cataract operation to repair the damage.

So, life for political prisoners was made as uncomfortable as possible. But they did not take all this abuse lying down. After the powerful and proud leadership figures arrived on the island, the prisoners began to organize themselves and embarked on a series of hunger strikes and legal challenges to force the prison authorities to improve conditions. These periodic protests, along with the horrific reports from those prisoners who had been released, grabbed the attention of the media and international organizations such as the United Nations, Amnesty International and the Red Cross. As a result, the government reluctantly agreed to discipline or dismiss particularly egregious warders and superintendents. In 1978, Helen Suzman (a liberal member of parliament) visited the island and caused a stink about conditions in the prison, which also helped force the government's hand.

Thus, after the first major hunger strike in 1966, things gradually improved. In time, prisoners were allowed to read newspapers and books (censored, of course). They could even study for degrees through correspondence (although this was a privilege that could be taken away if a prisoner misbehaved). Sporting events between the prisoners were organized and cultural committees were set up. Soccer was particularly popular, which inspired the 2008 movie, *More than a Game*, about the island's Makana Football League. The resistance leaders also began working on the more sympathetic guards and engendered a less confrontational environment with the authorities to enable them to get what they wanted. Some of these warders even came to be sympathetic to the cause of the prisoners and helped sneak uncensored correspondence in and out of the prison. Once they became aware of this, however, the prison authorities made sure that all warders were white and regularly rotated them with other prisons so that they would not fall under the spell of the 'terrorists'.

Nevertheless, the confines of the island must have been unbearable for the prisoners. They were generally dynamic and committed people, most of whom were in the prime of their lives. Escape plans surfaced from time to time but none ever came to fruition. There was even one ambitious scheme whereby a helicopter would be flown to the island to snatch Mandela away, but this was quickly abandoned—perhaps at Madiba's insistence that he would only walk away as a free man and not as a fugitive.

The prisoners (who grew to about 1,000 in number) knew little of what was going on outside the prison walls. People living under the injustice of apartheid only knew of their leaders by name (since it was illegal to print or display images of banned people). Meanwhile, the whites made hay in the glorious South African sunshine, as blacks suffered from forced removals and institutionalized discrimination. The only bright point was when Verwoerd was assassinated by a slightly nutty sailor named Dimitri Tsafendas, in 1966. Yet through it all, the struggle continued.

The next big milestone occurred in 1976, when the government declared that henceforth the medium of education for all black students would be Afrikaans. This was a huge blow for black people who were already struggling to get a decent education, as well as a grievous insult—forcing students to learn in the language of their oppressors. By this time, a new kind of political ideology had become popular in the townships: black consciousness. Adopted and adapted from American resistance leaders such as Martin Luther King and Malcolm X, the tenet of black consciousness stated that black people should break free from the slave–master relationship and insist on being treated as equals in every sphere of life. It was a proud, principled and somewhat aggressive stance, epitomized by Steve Biko (who was arrested and murdered by the police in 1977).

Thus, in response to the hated Bantu Education Act, the students took matters into their own hands and young people across the country embarked on a series of protest actions. The most famous of these was the march of 15,000 students that took place on 16 June 1976 in the township of Soweto, adjacent to Johannesburg. Unsurprisingly, the police opened fire on the crowd and among the first to be killed was a young boy named Hector Petersen. The iconic photographs, taken by Sam Nzima, of a lifeless Hector being carried in the arms of his teenage relative became a clarion call to other disenchanted youth and a wave of unrest spread across the country. Today, we commemorate the Soweto uprising with a public holiday, Youth Day.

As before, the government's response was swift and unequivocal. Hundreds of student leaders and agitators were arrested and summarily sentenced to long prison terms on Robben Island. The prison population swelled to around 4,500, resulting in terrible overcrowding in a facility that was built to house 2,500. This new influx of young blood was a both blessing and a curse for the ageing 'old school' who had already spent over a decade in prison.

On the one hand, the young bloods brought with them welcome news from the outside world. On the other hand, however, the fiery students were filled with the exhortations of the black consciousness movement and dismissed the older prisoners' conciliatory approach to the guards as expediency. An ideological conflict between negotiation and confrontation subsequently flared up and tensions occasionally boiled over. This was exacerbated by a recruitment drive in which the leaders of the ANC and PAC tried to get the new kids on the block to ally themselves with one movement or the other. For a while, the unity of the prisoners was threatened. The astute elder-statesmen, however, managed to engage the new arrivals in debate and a reconciliation of sorts was achieved. So, even in the harsh environment of a prison, a culture of discussion and tolerance of contrary opinions prevailed. One can only hope that this culture is honoured by future political generations.

For the rest of the '70s and '80s, South Africa was balanced on a knife edge. The student uprising may have been put down, but protests and riots continued to be an almost daily occurrence in the townships. After B. J. Vorster was forced to resign as prime minister in 1978 as a result of a financial scandal, a humourless, dangerous megalomaniac named P. W. Botha took over the reigns of government. PW wagged his finger and instituted an endless series of raids and arrests. For the next ten years, South Africa would be run as a police state under a general state of emergency which gave the security forces extraordinary powers. Prisoners could be detained without trial for months at a time. The press was heavily censored. The police and army prowled the townships in fearsome vehicles, such as Casspirs, firing bullets and teargas at anything that looked like an illegal assembly. They were dark days indeed and the beloved country wept.

Then, quite suddenly, everything changed.

In 1986, several legislative pillars of apartheid were

repealed, such as the Mixed Marriages Act and the much-hated Pass Laws. In 1988, South Africa withdrew from South West Africa/Namibia (mandated to South Africa at the end of World War I, but repealed by the United Nations in the 1960s). Finally, in 1990, to the surprise and joy of most people, opposition parties such as the ANC and PAC were unbanned and Mandela was released.

The reasons for this remarkable about-face are still somewhat difficult to fathom, but it was doubtless a combination of different factors that made the government come to its senses. Among other things, these factors include—relentless international pressure in the form of sanctions; exclusion from organizations such as the United Nations, the Olympics and the Commonwealth; and a plummeting local currency. The final death knell for apartheid was when the old tyrant, P. W. Botha, was pushed out of power by his own party which was becoming increasingly embarrassed by his erratic behaviour and hard-line policies. The man who took over from was F. W. de Klerk, and he deserves full credit for pushing through many major reforms against considerable resistance from his supporters. Perhaps he and his party had finally realized that the government could simply not hold back the flood gates of black political aspirations any longer, and chose to follow a path of negotiation rather than a path of civil war. In any event, the years from 1990 until the first democratic elections of 1994 were historic. There were months of hard-fought negotiations and right-wing attempts to destabilize the country. Finally, and against the odds, a voluntary handover of power was achieved. Often called the first 'peaceful revolution', it was the beginning of a new era in South African history.

Although it seemed to us that everything changed almost overnight, the reality is a little bit more complex. Mandela and the other Rivonia trialists were actually moved off Robben Island back in 1982 and sent to Pollsmoor Prison on the mainland. Here they were allowed to meet with representatives of the government and business, who were looking for a way out of the mess that they had spawned. Several times the leadership were given the option of going free if they publicly denounced the armed struggle and each time they stated that they would only do so if the government did the same.

The stalemate continued until 1988, when Mandela was moved to a house in the grounds of the Victor Verster Prison. By this time, the winds of change were gusting across the sub-continent and Mandela was again offered his freedom. He refused once more and insisted that his colleagues be released first, knowing that the crafty government might refuse to release the others once the ANC's figurehead was free. Accordingly, one by one, the other political leaders were abruptly released with little fanfare and no warning. And finally, on 2 February 1990, the world watched as Madiba and Winnie walked hand in hand through the gates of Victor Verster and into the light.

Following this momentous event, the remaining political prisoners on Robben Island were left in a state of confusion and excitement. Rumours swirled around the prison and the government, rather cruelly, refused to issue any conclusive statement on the issue. Gradually, however, they were all granted their freedom and unceremoniously released, with no counselling and no support, back into society.

The manner of their release is still recalled with bitterness by some former prisoners. Many of the detainees returned to shattered families and broken lives. They were given no compensation for their time in prison and few had prospects for employment. A number of ex-political prisoners subsequently turned to alcohol and substance abuse. Even today, there is still no substantial programme to assist those who wasted their youths in the jails of apartheid and, while the perpetrators of the Nationalist system continue to live comfortable lives, the foot soldiers of the struggle have been left with nothing.

By 1991, all political prisoners had left Robben Island. It continued to serve as a prison for criminal prisoners until 1996, when it was finally decided to close the place down and relocate the remaining captives to mainland facilities. The fate of Robben Island was once again unclear.

Thankfully, by this time, the importance of the island as a symbol of the struggle and as an icon of victory over injustice was being recognized. The decision was taken to turn the entire island into a museum that would educate people about the evils of racism and the power of tolerance. The Robben Island Museum officially opened on 1 January 1997. In 1999, this initiative was endorsed by the international community when the island was inscribed into the World Heritage List.

Today, thousands of people visit the former prison every week to experience for themselves the miraculous story of Robben Island. It is not always a pleasant pilgrimage, but it is one that we should all undertake so that the painful lessons of the past 500 years are not forgotten. By keeping the memory of Robben Island we may, for once, prevent history from repeating itself.

Exclusive interview with Matlakana Philemon Tefu—former political prisoner, incarcerated on Robben Island from 1964 to 1985

DF: Where did you grow up?

MPT: I was born in 1940, and I grew up in Pretoria, in a township called Riverside. Next to Riverside, there was a poor white area that is still there now—East Lynne. The two areas were divided by a little jungle and we used to hunt birds there. Whenever we'd meet with the folks from the white section, we would either beat them or they would beat us [*laughs*]. So, in a way, that contributed to my attitude. Later, around 1954 we moved to Mamelodi because of those forced removals. I stayed in Mamelodi from 1954, right up to the time I was arrested in 1963.

DF: Were you always aware of politics or did something happen to make you aware of it?

MPT: Well, as you grow up, you gain awareness. You ask things such as, 'Whose country is this?' And the parents say that 'It belongs to the government.' And you ask, 'Who is the government?' And they say, 'Oh, it's whites.' Then, when something happens that you don't like, they say, 'No, it's the government.' So you tend to hate that which is called the government, and the government is white.

DF: Did your parents accept the situation?

MPT: My parents had accepted; resigned themselves to the situation. For instance, my father belonged to the school of thought that said a black person is dependant upon a white person.

I remember one incident later, in 1962, when I was deeply involved in politics. I saw two whites sort of quarrelling with a black man. And I got involved. But it was no longer a spontaneous thing, it was now nationalism. It was politically motivated. It was conscious. I don't remember what happened, but when I went home, my shirt was torn and I had a blue eye.

The next morning, my father said ... well, to him I was now a child who has gone off the path. So he called me in to set me right. And he said that a black man's medicine is a white man. I said, 'No, that [attitude] is yours. It's not me. I don't belong to that.' Then he became resigned. You know, when a father resigns in that way, you are no longer his son—you are the mother's son.

DF: How did you first get involved in the PAC?

MPT: With me, I was political before I actually joined the PAC. Around 1958, I had a teacher who implanted some politics. At that same time, Ghana had just gained its independence, and we heard about this black person who was a prime minister. The question of a black prime minister was, at that time, unthinkable. So, when you are told that there is a black prime minister ... that showed us a new dawn.

I left school after standard six and went to find work. I was very interested in African politics so, every day, I'd buy a *Rand Daily Mail* in the morning and *The Star* in the afternoon. The train was still the prime means of transport then. So, in the train, I'd read the newspapers and have conversations with people.

Then, there was this guy. He happened to work close to me. So, from Pretoria station right down to Struben Street, we'd walk together, walk and talk, and he learned of my state of mind. He subsequently approached me and said,

'Look there is an organization. We intend going for white-killing.' And I said, 'Put me there.' That was my response—'Put me there.'

Well, we then started organizing because there was a call to start an uprising against the whites. We were going to go into the white suburbs with our *pangas* [machetes] and just move them out. But we had to organize Mamelodi and establish branches. We were still organizing when we were arrested.

DF: Tell us about the arrest.

MPT: Well, this was now 1963, and the PAC was banned. This meant we were exposed, but that didn't stop us. We forged ahead. So it was easy, I believe, for the special branch to become aware of us. Then the police came in the morning of 22 March 1963, and they collected us. We had just come from a Sharpeville commemoration service. It ended somewhere around 23:00, so we just had a two hours' sleep when the police came. We were taken to Silverton police station that very night.

Our awaiting trial was from 22 March up to 17 June. And our trial was very fast. It took just a week—we were sentenced on 22 June. There were three life sentences. It just took a week.

DF: And when the trial was happening, did you know they were going to put you away?

MPT: Ja, we knew. Even when they found us guilty, we saluted. And the police said *'Gots, hulle salute nog!'* [Hell, they're still saluting!]

DF: How did you get to Robben Island?

MPT: Well, we were handcuffed, both legs and hands, and loaded into trucks. Then we drove to Cape Town. You were handcuffed to a partner, so whenever nature called, you had to take your colleague with you. At Cape Town, we were loaded into the basement of these boats. Some of us got seasick.

DF: Tell us about a typical day on the island.

MPT: Well, in the early days, the cells had a bucket system for a toilet. Moving out in the morning, you had to pick up your hands like this [*raises his hands above his head*]. They used to call it 'surrendering'. And then they searched you, and when the warders told you to turn that way or this way, they gave you a good slap on the face. So, you started your day like that.

Then you moved to get your dish of soft porridge and you went to some open place where you were going to squat and eat. You were not allowed to sit down. They would say '*Sit op jou agter-poote*' [Sit on your haunches], and we'd sit like this [*MPT squats down on his haunches*].

After eating, you went to your *span* [team]. When you came back, they searched you—strip-searched you. You would have to strip naked and turn over each item of your clothing to your warder. Then you'd have to turn around to show them that you weren't hiding anything in your anus. Then, you went to collect your food and you went to that same open space to squat, like before. But in about December of 1963, I think, Colonel Wessels stopped that.

DF: Tell us a bit about the warders.

MPT: There were warders that I'd say had a little intelligence. But generally they were outright sadists, like the Kleynhans brothers. Just sadists. I think the atmosphere was conducive to the production of sadists.

DF: If you could see them today, would you say anything to them?

MPT: No, just laugh at them. '*Ja, jong* …' [Yes, you people …].

DF: How did the warders treat you?

MPT: I was put on the *landbou-span* [agriculture team]. But, really, there was no sense to it, because we were just taking sand from this place to that place, using wheelbarrows and our backs ... for nothing, really. And it was really bad there. It was, I would say, the hardest of the labour sections at Robben Island.

They had criminals [on the *span*], that's common-law prisoners, and the warders would set them on us. These criminals were called *agter-ryers* [literally behind-riders]. They worked behind us to chase us and beat us.

Sometimes the warders would make you dig a trench, and then they would make you go in there and they would cover you in sand, so only your head and face showed. Then the warder would take out his penis and shower you with urine. That's what used to happen there.

Later on, we had things such as *bougroep* [building group], *klipgroep* [stone/quarry group] and so on, but *landbou* was the worst because it was actually a punishment *span*. The quarry was not so bad, because you're extracting stones from nature, so there is some purpose. But with the *landbou* it was purposeless, simply punishment.

After Commandant Oukamp left, things got better. The warders were told they were not allowed to hit us anymore. But there was one *rooikoppie* [red-headed] prison guard and he would say, '*Hulle sê ons moet hulle nie slaan nie, maar hulle sê nie ons moet hulle nie skop nie.*' [They say we aren't allowed to hit them, but they don't say we aren't allowed to kick them.]

And then there was a head warder, Zille. He used to kick us a lot and we complained to the jailer, named Theron. So he went to Zille and said, '*Zille, hoekom skop jy my bandiete?*' [Zille, why are you kicking my convicts?] And Zille said, '*Nee, ek het hulle nie geskop nie.*' [No, I didn't kick them.] And Theron said, '*Ek's nie 'n volstruis nie. Hoekom skop jy my bandiete?*' [I'm not an ostrich. Why do you kick my convicts?] And Zille said, '*Nee, ek het hulle nie geskop nie. Ek het hulle net getik.*' [I didn't kick them. I just gave them a little tap.]

At times, we'd complain about the mielie meal. You know mielie meal, when it is kept for a long time, it will get little worms. And when we complained, the warder would say that, 'You complain about getting too little meat. Well, that's meat, that's protein.' [*laughs*] But that was Robben Island.

DF: Did you have to call the warders 'baas' [boss]?

MPT: The PAC Status Campaign was largely that of not calling them 'baas'. We'd call them 'mister', in Afrikaans, *meneer*. It was a continuation of the Defiance Campaign. And they'd say, '*Gots, daar's vir jou 'n kaffir.*' [Hell, that's a kaffir for you.] And they'd say, '*Meneer is 'n kaffir predikant. Ek is 'n baas vir jou.*' ['Mister' is a kaffir teacher. I am 'boss' to you.]

DF: When Mandela and the big names arrived after Rivonia Trial, did things change?

MPT: They arrived on Robben Island in 1964. We had already been there over 12 months. And, at that time, the *boers* were still … they were still *boers*. So no, there wasn't any particular or visible change that came. I mean, they were treated in the same way as the other prisoners, except they were segregated as the *leiers* [leaders].

DF: Was there rivalry between the prisoners and the different political parties, such as the ANC and PAC?

MPT: On the island, there was some peaceful co-existence between PAC and ANC, but understand that during the '60s, PAC was predominant, numerically. And I'd say also qualitatively. But we would co-operate with the ANC and most of the hunger strikes were jointly organized.

DF: Were you involved in the sports activities?

MPT: There were two leading teams, like Kaiser Chiefs and Pirates. They were the Vultures and the Gunners. I was the fullback for the Gunners, a very powerful one. The sports were good.

DF: Twenty years is a long time to be in prison. How did you cope, mentally?

MPT: I'd say that, what kept us going was a commitment to the struggle. That's why it was so important to get information about what was happening outside, particularly regarding the struggle. And we still believed that freedom would come very, very soon—a matter of three or four years. It was Japhta Masemola who said, 'No man, 1980, you'll find us here.' And we said, 'Nah, this old guy, he's saying this because he's married already.'

But you dream. I used to dream on the island, that I was sentenced to death. And when you realize that it's a dream, it's a relief. At the same time, you know, you'll also dream that you're on your way home and your girlfriend is waiting to greet you. But when you wake up, the first thing that you see are those grills over the window, and they tell you that you are in prison.

DF: You weren't married when you were arrested. Does that make it easier or harder?

MPT: I think it was good [I was not married] because others, they cried. But it depends, because some people, like me, got into our minds that, '*Sponono diege, sebenza lisiswe.*' In other words, 'Pretty girl, leave me so that I can serve the nation.' One might think that we were taking drugs, but it was not drugs. We were just made to understand what it means to be a liberator, to be ready to die. Once you accepted it, that was your role. That was your purpose. We would actually sing that we want a no-return assignment. Some people said that we were tools of history.

DF: You were released from Robben Island in 1985, and you remained active in politics until the 1994 elections, when the PAC won only five seats. Then you decided to leave politics. Why?

MPT: Well, it was most unfortunate with my peer group, the 1963 lot. We did not aspire to become leaders. We were simply foot soldiers. To me it was just service, and when I was not elected … well, sometimes history chooses you to be in that position and sometimes it drops you. It may call you back.

DF: How does it feel to talk about the island now? Is it still painful?

MPT: It's not bad. I don't feel any pain.

DF: Are you angry?

MPT: No, I'm not angry. I'm not angry about where I come from. I'm not angry about the past. I might be angry about the present. You see what is happening today in Africa, in Zimbabwe, and realize that things might take longer than the long walk to freedom of Mandela.

DF: Are you proud of your contribution?

MPT: Yes, I'm proud but not, say, fulfilled. I'm happy that, now, we can sit and have coffee and talk like this. That wasn't always the case. But we have not achieved the Pan-Africanist ideal. The West still wants Africa divided so that it can keep on looting.

DF: So you don't like the West?

MPT: It is the West that enslaved us; it is the West that colonized us; it is the West that is neo-colonizing us. So I don't think that will make me like the West.

DF: Do you believe that people can change?

MPT: Well, yes. For instance, there was Reverend Shaffers who held church services on Robben Island. He used to say to us, 'You smoke *dagga* [marijuana] and get drunk and think about freedom, that's why you are in prison.' But he changed, very radically, to the point where, at one time, he used to smuggle in newspapers. And he was from the Dutch Reformed Church! He actually said that he's not going to be like those of the Russian Church, I think, who were counting money while the revolution was raging outside. He was not going to be like that. He had changed from a *verkrampte* [conservative] Afrikaner.

DF: And now you live in Pretoria and speak Afrikaans.

MPT: I do speak Afrikaans, but it's Afrikaans like they spoke it on Robben Island. You know that prison way of speaking? Like, '*Wat die donder is die?*' [What the hell is this?] You know, in 1997 I went up Table Mountain and, when I looked at Robben Island, I said, '*Ooh God, daar's daaie donderse Robben Island,*' [Oh God, there's that bloody Robben Island], speaking more or less the same as those warders. And this old warder was also there and he heard me, so he came over to me, and I knew him and he knew me too. And we laughed about it.

DF: So now, when you see white people, you don't automatically see *boere*?

MPT: No, now it's a different story. In fact, I think the Afrikaners would be very happy if they were to listen to me talking today because I believe that they are Africa's adopted sons and daughters. I mean, the Afrikaners have no homeland outside Africa, so Africa has to be their home. We can talk about the English and their homeland in England, but not the Afrikaners. So I strongly believe that they are Africa's adopted sons and daughters.

DF: So the past is the past?

MPT: Ja, the past is the past. It doesn't do to mourn the past. Rather look to the future and try to improve it. But the future needs to be much better than how it presents itself at the moment. We must shape the future in such a way that we all benefit and live together.

Fauna and flora

Robben Island is a wild place. It is terribly hot in summer and freezing cold in winter. When the wind picks up speed, as it so often does in Cape Town, a gale howls over the little hump of rock and makes the island seem forlorn and forbidding. Before the arrival of humans on the island, the native vegetation consisted mainly of grasses and some low shrubs. All the trees that can be seen today were planted by humans in the last 500 years in an effort to make the island more homely.

One of the reasons for this vegetative paucity is that the island has never had a good water supply. There are no rivers or streams, just a few brackish pools of water. When humans arrived, water was always in short supply and houses were usually built with large tanks to collect the rain water. In the twentieth century, a desalination plant was installed to improve the water supply, but it is still a thirsty place for those creatures which cannot live in sea water.

The native fauna originally consisted mainly of aquatic animals, such as seals, sea birds and penguins. Mole snakes are also indigenous to the island. All the other animals that now live on the island were introduced by humans. Today, these interlopers include about 15 springbok, 100 steenbok, 200 European fallow deer, a couple of bontebok, an eland and a few ostriches. There are also lots of rabbits, rats and feral cats. Consequently, the small island is now overpopulated and the recently approved Integrated Conservation Management Plan (ICMP) includes a provision to reduce the number of fallow deer, cats and other undesirables. A controversial rabbit cull got underway in 2008, which caught and euthanized 2,205 animals in six weeks. The rabbit-reduction programme will switch to a sterilization strategy when the population becomes more stable. By comparison, the ICMP seeks to support native species by building nest boxes for penguins and clearing the island of alien vegetation.

In any case, the island is teeming with wildlife. Rabbits skitter through the shrubs and buck roam free across the blessedly unfenced land. When I stayed overnight, I opened the curtains of the guesthouse and saw several *bokkies* (buck) calmly grazing on the lawn. Even when you don't see them, there is evidence of animals everywhere. *Drolletjies* (buck droppings) dot the rugby field and penguin guano streaks the road, creating informal penguin crossings. Birdlife also abounds and around 74 species of birds, including cormorants, seagulls and lapwings, thrive along the uninhabited stretch of coast.

Most noticeable, however, are the African penguins. They throng the shore close to the harbour and go where they please. I was even startled by a penguin which darted out of the bushes inside the prison, while I was on my way to Mandela's cell. One long-time resident of the island who has been living there for over 20 years says that, in the old days, the penguins were less cocky because they knew that they would wind up in the pot of a hungry prison warder. Now, they are taking over the island and it is estimated that around 13,000 of the little critters live there.

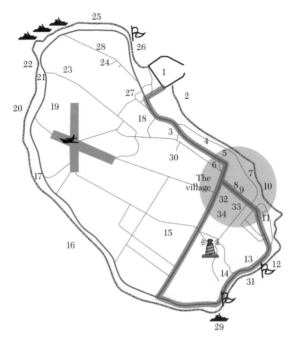

Highlighted area represents the bus route

⚐ lookouts
➤ landing strip
⚓ shipwrecks
🗼 Minto Hill and lighthouse

1. Harbour
2. Murray's Bay
3. Old leper cemetries
4. Site of male leper quarters
5. Robert Sobukwe's house
6. Church of the Good Shepherd
7. Old criminal prison
8. Old leper morgue
9. Garrison Church
10. Faure jetty
11. Commissioner's house
   (guesthouse)
12. Ladies' Rock/Alpha One
13. Van Riebeeck quarry
14. WWII barrack ruins
15. De Waal Battery
16. Long Bay
17. Bath of Bethesda

18. Maximum-security prison
19. Stone quarry
20. Shelley Beach
21. Blue slate quarry
22. Rangatira Bay
23. Ruins of female and child leper
   quarters
24. Old prison
25. Seal colony
26. Penguin boardwalk
27. Kramat
28. Cornelia Battery
29. *Fong Chung 11* 1977
30. Limestone quarry
31. Edmond's Pool
32. Barracks
33. School
34. General Infirmary cemetery

Indeed, there is a sense that Robben Island remains stubbornly untamed. Human beings have tried to 'civilize' it by planting palm trees (now bent by the wind) and cultivating bright bougainvillea in the dusty gardens. But the island is still something of a blasted heath and that's all part of its rugged beauty.

Visiting Robben Island

Thankfully, access to Robben Island is no longer restricted and modern tourists can visit the island all year round. What follows is a step-by-step guide to the modern Robben Island tour. Please be advised, however, that you must book your place in advance to avoid disappointment. Price details, phone numbers and departure times all appear at the end of this book.

The V&A Waterfront

As a tourist, your journey to Robben Island begins at the Victoria and Alfred Waterfront. This is a busy retail hub, bursting with shops, restaurants, cinemas and Germans. The bustling complex sprawls over a large area and, depending upon your proclivities, you can spend a good few hours browsing the shops before or after your trip to the island.

Originally an industrial dockyard and harbour for the city of Cape Town, the nineteenth-century waterfront area fell into disuse after larger docks were built on the foreshore in the twentieth century. Then, in 1988, the decaying warehouses were refurbished to create the sparkling new Waterfront that we enjoy today. In addition to a large, enclosed shopping mall, called Victoria Wharf, the complex spreads across the Victoria Basin, offering fantastic harbour views. Pleasure cruises and helicopter flips are available, but none of these will take you to Robben Island.

For that you must make your way to the Nelson Mandela Gateway, where you catch the Robben Island ferry. The Gateway and jetty are situated at the mouth of the compact

Alfred Basin, where you will find several upmarket hotels and private yachts basking in the sun. The view of Table Mountain from the Alfred Basin is marvellous. The Gateway also stands next to the Clock Tower, a bright-red landmark, and both are clearly signposted throughout the Waterfront.

If you park in one of the main parking lots near the mall, remember that you will have quite a long walk to the Gateway. But you'll also have the pleasure of crossing a delicate swing bridge, which spans the narrow channel between the Alfred Basin and the sea. The best place to park, therefore, is in the Clock Tower Centre, located on the far side of the Waterfront complex. This parkade is a bit tricky to find, as it's only accessible from the main roundabout near the city, but it will bring you out right at the Gateway building.

In addition to the Gateway, the Clock Tower Centre also contains dozens of shops and restaurants. It has a large, well-staffed tourist information centre upstairs, with representatives from all over the country. This is an excellent source for information on Cape Town, the Western Cape and the whole of South Africa. The Info Centre has an internet café and you can book your tickets for the Robben Island tour at the main desk.

The Nelson Mandela Gateway

The striking, geometric design of the Gateway building is unmistakable. Head up the broad stone stairs and walk through the tall, glass doors, and your journey to Robben Island has begun. In front of you is the info desk, staffed by several amazingly patient people who answer the same three questions over and over again—the ferry leaves every two hours from 09:00. The tour takes about four hours. To your left is the gift shop, where you can buy an amazing range of Robben Island merchandise. Branded 'RI' mineral water, socks, scarves, key rings, bookmarks, diaries, mouse pads, calendars, spoons, glasses, shirts, earrings, mugs,

ISLAND TOUR

jackets, postcards, fridge magnets and facsimile copies of the Freedom Charter are all available. You can even buy a key to Robben Island, which is rather appropriate since that is exactly what the old prisoners would've wanted for Christmas. The shop also has a good selection of books and videos, including an activity book for kids.

The ticket office is on your right. If you have been wise enough to book ahead, you will collect your tickets here. It is always busy at the ticket window, so arrive early to avoid stress. You can also buy your tickets at the window, but don't think that you can just arrive and get on the next ferry out. About half a million people visit the island every year, and the ferry only takes 300 people at a time. So it is unsurprising that the tours are usually booked up a day or two in advance. In the high season, over December and January, bookings are very scarce indeed.

Although most people only think of the Gateway as the place where you get your tickets, the building is an integral part of the museum experience. There are several exhibitions on the upper floors and an extensive video archive through which you can browse. Visitors who rush through the Gateway will miss out on a lot, so arrive early and spend some time exploring.

The building has three levels. On the entrance level, which is in the middle, there is a video-mural installation. It consists of video messages from a wide range of ex-political prisoners, both from Robben Island and other prisons.

On the upper level, there are several exhibition spaces and the searchable video archives. When I was last there, there was an excellent exhibition called 'Media in Struggle', which contained hundreds of posters from the anti-apartheid movement. While walking around this display, it struck me as both fascinating and sad. There are so many people whom we are slowly forgetting, and there are many others whose names we never learned. All the material that makes up these exhibits is sourced from the Robben Island-Mayibuye

Archive, held at the University of the Western Cape. On the lower level, there are several large, evocative photographs of the island and its former prisoners, as well a collection of wooden cabinets. Open the draws of these cabinets and you will see an eclectic assortment of relics from the island—shackles, prisoners' letters, threadbare prison blankets, home-made certificates from sporting events and other personal effects. The lower level also has an auditorium that is used for special events and staff meetings (which I'm told can be quite energetic, as is appropriate for an organization with its roots in the liberation movement).

Once you are finished looking around, you should proceed to the lower level where you will board the ferry. Boarding starts 30 minutes prior to departure—and departure is always on time.

The ferry ride

A highlight of the tour is the actual boat ride over to the island. The ferry takes about 30 minutes each way and the views of Cape Town and Table Mountain are superb. Take along plenty of film (or memory cards) because the scene keeps on changing and you'll want to take another picture every few minutes. At times, the ferry looks like a porcupine, bristling with cameras and cellphones as passengers try to capture the collosal vista. Video cameras are also prevalent and every journey of the ferry is captured in its entirety by at least a dozen videographers—making it probably the most documented boat ride in the world.

The modern high-speed ferry is quite smooth, gliding over the swells with confidence. If you do suffer from sea sickness however, take your pills because the crossing can be rough. But don't let this stop you from making the trip. It's well worth a bit of nausea.

In order to improve the service, a smart new three-tier ferry, named *Sikhululekile* (we are free) was launched in February 2008. It carries 300 passengers at a top speed of 27 knots and has six public toilets! Built specifically for the Robben Island Museum at a cost of some R26 million, this sleek craft replaced to the two aging 160-seater ferries, *Autshumato* and *Makana*, which were run by an external company. Between them, these old twin-hull ferries covered nearly 550,000km during their nine years in Table Bay. They now ply the azure waters of the Caribbean. Unfortunately, there was a delay between the decommissioning of the old ferries and delivery of the new one, and two smaller apartheid-era vessels had to be recruited into temporary service: the *Dias* and the *Susan Kruger* (named after the wife of Jimmy Kruger, the infamous Minister of Police who once said that the death of Steve Biko "leaves me cold").

Two chartered craft, the *Penguin* and the *Sea Princess*, were also brought in to take up the slack. While the other vessels are now out of service, the *Susan Kruger* was recently refurbished and is still being used as a secondary passenger ferry. The island's cargo ferry, the *Blouberg*, was also improved as part of the upgrade programme. Even though the new *Sikhululekile* ferry is double the size of the old ones, it only does about half the number of trips a day, so it's always full. This results in a bit of pushing and shoving, particularly when the swells are high and people stagger from one side of the boat to the other in order to take in the view. However, plans to purchase a second 300-seater ferry have been put on hold.

The *Sikhululekile* has a kiosk which sells sandwiches, snacks and drinks, but hot food is not prepared on the boat. You may bring your own food and drink on board, but alcoholic beverages are not permitted.

In any event, after a fantastic journey across the channel from Cape Town, the ferry docks at Murray's Harbour on Robben Island. Visitors then disembark and walk past towering black and white pictures of the island's past, toward the waiting buses.

The bus tour

After enjoying the privilege of walking around the island by myself, I must confess that the bus trip is the least fulfilling part of the tour. This is not because the well-trained bus guides are bad. Indeed, they are excellent and must complete a six-month training course before they are allowed to take tourists around. But, unavoidably, the bus does not stop anywhere for long and you are not allowed to get off the bus to explore.

This is quite understandable. There is only a limited time available and a large number of people to process. Furthermore, there is a community of 150 people living on the island and their lives would be greatly disrupted by a constant stream of strangers strolling through their village. As it is, the buses drive past with such regularity that the local children walking home from school have grown accustomed to the stream of gawking faces that peer out of the passing windows.

In the future, the Robben Island Museum is planning to inaugurate a walking tour of the island and, perhaps, a mountain-bike route. When these become available, I would heartily recommend that you take up the offer. You really have to tread on the soil of Robben Island to experience the power of the place. Later in this book you will find a more complete description of the local community and my unofficial walking tour around the island. For the moment, however, we are stuck on the bus; this is what you'll see …

Leaving the harbour, you pass through the concrete portals that bear the island emblem (a lily) and the apartheid-era prison motto, 'We serve with pride. Ons dien met trots'. A slightly sarcastic 'Welcome' is also painted down the side of the entranceway.

A military gun post from World War II is briefly visible to your left, with the main bulk of the maximum-security prison looming up ahead. The bus continues to the left, dodging the penguins, and soon pulls up alongside an old cemetery, quite close to the prison walls. This is the old lepers' cemetery and the crumbling graves seem to ring with the pathos of their mournful inhabitants.

The next stop is Robert Sobukwe's house, set a short distance away from the village. The tiny two-roomed house looks very small to have housed a big personality like Sobukwe, but it was here that he lived for nine years with almost no human contact. The dog kennels alongside the house were added in 1976, after the Soweto uprising, when additional attack dogs were brought in to help subdue the feisty new arrivals.

The bus continues on to the Church of the Good Shepherd. This simple, whitewashed structure was designed by Sir Herbert Baker as a place of worship for the people living with leprosy, who were then resident at the General Infirmary. It had no pews and very small windows, so that the disease wouldn't infect the other islanders. It was built in 1895 and is a national monument.

You now drive through the village, also known as Irish Town. It is a mixed bag of buildings. Some date from the Victorian era when the island was a hospital, others date from the military years during the Second World War. There are also several newer structures built for the community of warders who lived here with their families when it was still an apartheid prison. These later buildings tend to be as humourless and as dull as the Nationalist politicians of the time, and the compound built for the unmarried white guards is particularly horrible (although still much better than a prison cell).

As part of their commitment to heritage management and preservation, the museum keeps all the buildings on Robben Island in a more-or-less original condition. The paint is permitted to peel and renovations are not allowed, apart from those improvements which are necessary to keep the buildings standing. This is entirely appropriate for a museum, but it does make life somewhat unusual for the people who live and work here. The admin building, for example, is built around an unpainted concrete courtyard and is still strongly reminiscent of the old prison offices that they once were. Even in the village, things are not allowed to be changed. The old asylum for female lunatics still stands, empty and abandoned, shrieking with mute misery.

Today, the village is home to 150 permanent residents. They consist of museum staff, prison guides, National Ports Authority employees, lighthouse keepers, Works Department personnel and a couple of die-hards from the old days. It is a small and isolated community but it is enchanting. The children walk freely to each other's houses, doors are left unlocked and time slows down to the point of irrelevance. Rather like Canada.

The village contains about 100 houses, arranged in broad strips on either side of the main road. Each home has a dusty garden and a barrel for catching rain water. Only 40 of them are currently inhabited, which makes the island rather spooky at night. Charlé, the postmistress, told me that she handles 2,000 letters a month, and the island's post office wins awards for its efficiency. The turreted Anglican church, now Dutch Reformed, still has church services twice a month. In the centre of the village is the *Ledewinkel* or community store. The locals get their supplies here and the kids drive the shopkeeper mad by constantly nagging for free sweets. The broad *stoep* (verandah) of the shop also functions as a meeting place, with two plastic tables provided for afternoon chats.

Next to the shop are a playground and an incongruous miniature-golf course (what South Africans call Putt-Putt or Adventure Golf). It was built for the prison warders' entertainment and it's still in pretty good nick. A large swimming pool, behind a high wall, is where the kids usually spend their afternoons, sunning themselves on the warm concrete and pushing each other into the water. The village also has a rugby field and a surreal cricket pitch, which was originally built by the British (who else).

The island has a crèche and primary school, with 23 kids and two teachers. There is no high school, so older children either have to move to Cape Town or catch the daily staff ferry to the mainland. This can be a difficult commute, however, and there is one story of a matric pupil who couldn't get to his final exam because the sea was too rough. Apparently, the Air Force sent a helicopter to get him!

At the southern end of the village, facing the hazy shore of Bloubergstrand, is the Governor's residence and the parsonage. These comparatively grand buildings date from the Victorian era and now house the conference centre and the guesthouse (which is only open to invited guests).

Once past the village, the road swings to the right and runs across the southern edge of the island, right along the coastline. The view is jaw-dropping. Across the channel, Table Mountain, Devil's Peak and Lion's Head rise up with preternatural force, dominating the island. As you drive, the guide will point out Van Riebeeck's old quarry, several WWII rifle posts, the demolished military barracks, concrete WWII lookouts and a recent shipwreck (the *Fong Chung No. 11*, which ran aground in 1975). You'll also pass Alpha One, a recreational venue and lookout built during the apartheid years. Although it is currently unused, Alpha One has a braai area with one of the best views on the planet.

Unfortunately, the bus now turns off the perimeter road and drives up the modest slope of Minto Hill, toward the lighthouse. Buck can usually be seen grazing on the thick grass at the foot of the hill, which soon gives way to a dense gum-tree plantation. At the crest of the hill stands the lighthouse. Built in 1865, it has a range of 24 sea miles and a 1.5kW lamp. Its light gives one flash of five seconds' duration every seven seconds. It is the modern descendant of the signal fires that the Dutch used to light on this very same spot, over 300 years ago. A radar station, the De Waal gun battery and a water desalination plant (which supplies the island with fresh water) are all close to the lighthouse. The bus continues over the hill, past the once-planned golf course (!) and back into the village. At the top of the town, just visible from the road, is a second cemetery that contains the graves of officers and doctors who worked at the General Infirmary. Once you are back in the village, the bus turns left and heads to the maximum-security prison.

The prison tour

After the bus tour, visitors are deposited at the entrance of the maximum-security prison for the emotional and rather distressing prison tour. This part of your visit is guided by 'genuine' ex-political prisoners and their personal insights make the walk through the prison both memorable and chilling.

Unlike the bus guides, the prison guides do not have an extensive training session and are not given a specific script to follow. Nevertheless, I am told that most of the prisoners have shared a common experience and their interpretations of life in the jail tend to be similar and equally powerful. I asked my guide, Derrick Basson, what it was like to return to the prison as a guide and his answer was quite forthright. At first, he admitted, it was difficult to come back and confront the past. Now, he's starting to enjoy it. He feels as if he is making a contribution to nation-building by educating people about apartheid and sharing the lessons we have learned. He is also eager to show international visitors that they too have their own problems with racism and that these issues need to be dealt with in their own countries. After all, the problems of apartheid don't end at our borders and the evil of racist thinking in found right across the world.

Derrick also said that he and most of the other ex-prisoners who returned to work on the island, did so because they were unemployed and needed work. He didn't feel it was the kind of thing that someone would give up a job to come and do—it was necessity rather than ideology that brought people back to the prison. Derrick then reminded me that most of the prisoners were released without any kind of counselling, compensation or prospect of employment, which must have been a bitter pill to swallow.

And the prison guides work hard. There are currently about 15 former political prisoners on the island and, in peak season, they can do up to six tours a day. This is bound to get exhausting and monotonous, kind of like an office job. Derrick assures me that he finds something rewarding in every tour that he conducts and he doesn't mean the tips. It is, by the way, quite acceptable to give any of the guides a gratuity. The tour itself is somewhat flexible, but it will include most of the highlights described below:

From the outside, the maximum-security prison is a low, menacing building of dark stone. It is flanked by tall watchtowers that stand as sentinels on each corner of the complex. A dusty sports field, surrounded by a double fence topped with barbed wire, is situated on one side of the prison and this is where the inmates used to play their inter-prison league matches. The sports committees on Robben Island were very well organized, drawing up detailed minutes of their meetings and issuing certificates of participation to all the players.

Adjacent to the prison is the small kramat (shrine) of Sayed Adurohman Moturu, the Sheik of Madura. He was an Indonesian prince who was banished to Robben Island for fomenting political resistance against the Dutch East India Company. He died on the island in 1754. His body is now buried in Jakarta but Cape Muslims have been making the pilgrimage to his shrine for the past 250 years, even when the island was an apartheid prison. The current structure on the site was built in 1969 and a feast called the Khalifa is held here every year.

As you walk through the perimeter of rusting wire fences that surround the prison building, a feeling of sombre foreboding seems to rise up from the earth. Then, quite suddenly, you find yourself in jail. Your first stop is most likely to be the communal prison cells of Block A. Here, with all the visitors seated on benches arranged along the walls of the cell, your guide will tell you about living conditions inside the jail and will describe the various disciplinary regimes inflicted on the prisoners. Today the cells are empty and as cold as concrete, but one can acutely imagine the overcrowding and noise that once characterized this section. The bright but naïve murals on the walls of the cells do brighten things up a bit but these were only painted after 1991, when all the political prisoners had left.

From the communal cells, you are taken across a windswept courtyard, past various admin blocks, into the main prison building. This is where the hospital, censorship office and solitary cells for the political leadership were housed.

After walking down an echoing corridor, you are led out of a door and into a small concrete courtyard, surrounded by a high wall. This is the famous exercise yard where Mandela and the other 'dangerous' prisoners spent a few precious hours in the sunlight, before being put back into the adjoining solitary shoebox cells. The courtyard is now lined with large photographs of the famous personalities who were once incarcerated here but it remains a bleak place. It is no wonder that Mandela and others cultivated a small garden on one side of the yard in an effort to cheer things up.

After a short talk in the courtyard, in which the guide will describe how the isolated leaders managed to communicate with the other prisoners and the outside world through a complex smuggling network, the eager crowd heads off into B Section. This contains the row of solitary cells, arranged in pairs along a narrow corridor, lit by buzzing neon lights.

And now it's time for the main attraction: Cell 5, Block B. This is the tiny cubicle that contained one of the greatest figures of the twentieth century—Nelson Mandela. Our beloved Madiba lived here for 18 years, from 1964 to 1982, until he was transferred to a chalet on the grounds of

Pollsmoor Prison near Paarl. Visitors are allowed to file past the cell and take pictures, but photographs simply cannot express the claustrophobic confines of the cell. In fact, it is hard to fathom how anyone could emerge from this enclosed space with such an open heart. Mandela truly epitomizes the indomitable spirit of South Africa, as do all the other prisoners. We are lucky beyond imagining that they came out of incarceration with a generally positive outlook. It's also interesting to note that many of the first political leaders of a democratic South Africa went from prison into parliament, rather than the other way around.

After a ritualistic pilgrimage to The Cell, visitors are escorted out of the prison by their guide and directed back to the harbour, where they will catch the return ferry to Cape Town. In the short time you still have available, you can either browse the quayside shop or you can take a hurried stroll along the wooden boardwalk, which offers views of the penguins frolicking at the harbour's edge.

The ferry ride back to Cape Town is just as visually memorable as the ride out to the island. It is also a good time to sit back and reflect. Different people are bound to have different reactions to their time on Robben Island. Some may be pensive about their experience; others will be joyful that the prisoners' sacrifices have been validated with a happy ending. Then there are those who will simply knock back a beer and think about where to eat dinner.

But, whatever your response to the Robben Island tour, it remains an important rite of passage that should be undertaken by all South Africans and all citizens of the world. Even if you are only attracted by the celebrity of Mandela, try to open yourself up to the whole experience. It is a very emotional journey (several visitors have even had heart attacks while touring the island).

Once back at the Waterfront, the myriad delights of Cape Town beckon once more and the glories of a liberated South Africa are yours for the taking. But, before you dance into the clear light of our current democracy, spare a thought for the past. Although it is certainly tempting to forget about our painful history and concentrate only on the present that we are now enjoying, this would be a grave mistake. Only by remembering the long and tortured story of Robben Island will we ensure that the lessons, paid for so dearly with the blood of innocent people, are passed onto the next generation. And let us always recall the two very important words that are inscribed on the modern sculpture which stands at the entrance to Dachau and other Nazi concentration camps: *Plus jamais*—never again.

A walking tour of Robben Island

As mentioned, your time on Robben Island is limited and your bus tour around the island is restrictive. The best way to experience the real nature of the island is to walk it. I was lucky enough to be given the opportunity to do this for myself and I can honestly say that my walk around the island's perimeter was one of the most rewarding hikes of my life.

What follows, then, is a brief description of that walk. A complete circuit around the island is about 12 kilometres and it took me, at a leisurely walking pace, about four hours to complete. The perimeter of the island is totally flat and, apart from the hot sun, it is an easy and fulfilling stroll. We begin at the village.

The unique lifestyle of the local community is truly special. The quiet streets and houses, only half inhabited, bake in the sun as the scattered residents walk to and fro. There are very few private cars on the island, and regular staff-shuttles transport people around the island. For those employees who do not live on the island, a daily staff ferry is available and this is also used by island folk if they want to visit family or spend a weekend on the mainland. Housing in the village is generally free to employees but they have to apply for permission to live on the island.

There are currently about 150 people living on the island and they form a vibrant and fully functioning community. There is a local organization that represents the locals (RIVA—Robben Island Village Association) and there is even a bi-monthly island newsletter, called *The Lighthouse*.

It is rather surprising to see how many kids live on the island. Alice, who was my host, has two young children and she says that it's a great environment in which to raise a family. It's safe. It's sheltered from the urban decay of the modern world. And it's well equipped with sports facilities, a crèche and a canteen (which locals still call 'The Mess'). The school yard is a noisy, happy place and the local swimming pool (complete with lifeguard) is always busy.

It must be quite lonely, however, and rather insular—as any small community is bound to be. It's also very sleepy. While I was chatting to one of the locals, he let out a big yawn. Hoping it wasn't my conversation, I jokingly asked him if he was having that Friday feeling. He shrugged and simply replied, "No, that's life on the island."

At night, when the wind starts to howl, the island changes its face and becomes downright spooky. One of the local kids even tried to scare me with stories of ghosts that roam the dark streets. I totally believed him. If there's any place on Earth that is haunted by the phantoms of the past, it must be Robben Island. That evening, as I lay in bed, alone in the guesthouse, I thought that I could hear the restless movement of someone standing outside my window.

Nevertheless, the village is filled with a spirit of camaraderie. Everyone knows their neighbours and, apart from the occasional bit of island gossip, it is a warm and supportive environment. In the evenings, people either tend to stay home and watch TV or sit around in The Mess to chat, drink and talk politics.

Beyond the village, the first thing that strikes you is the view. There, across the channel, stands Table Mountain and all its brethren, resplendent in their glorious majesty. They seem so close, yet so far. This illusory proximity to Cape Town must have been torture for the prisoners. The view from the southern edge of the island is covered by the bus trip but you can't really appreciate the vista unless you slow down and drink in the scenery. I took full advantage of this luxury as I explored the Alpha One outpost, the *Fong Chung* shipwreck, the ruined army barracks, the abandoned WWII lookouts, and Van Riebeeck's old quarry (now filled with green water and frequented by water birds).

As you continue walking past the point where the bus turns away from the coast and up toward the lighthouse, you leave the 'civilized' part of the island behind and enter the wildness of the northwestern shore. Here, nature has been allowed to take over and the only sign of human interference is the narrow gravel road that leads along the serrated coast. The sound of the sea fills your senses, as birds gather in ever-increasing numbers on the jagged rocks. Buck graze quietly in the tall grass on the roadside. The solitude is total.

But the walk is never boring. From this vantage point, you can look right down the coast of the mainland: from the City Bowl to Sea Point, on to Camps Bay, along the Twelve Apostles to Chapman's Peak. It's a view you simply can't get from any other place on Earth.

There are also intriguing glimpses of the island's past along this forgotten promenade. There is the small white cross, at the edge of the sea, which commemorates the memory of Sergeant Bergselaar who drowned at this spot in 1955. A short distance farther along is a small boat house and the long-abandoned Bath of Bethesda—the tidal pool where the lepers used to bathe in the 'curative' cold sea water.

The island's landing strip now lies hidden behind a line of gum trees to the right, as the sea keeps up its constant vigil to the left. Ahead of you is only the open ocean. The silence is deafening. Near the top of the island, you come to the old slate quarry where many of the island's prisoners were subjected to back-breaking labour and spirit-breaking abuse. Today, the pit is filled with water that crashes over the broken sea wall, and the gulls react angrily to any human visitors who dare disturb their sanctuary. Rough mounds of broken stone stand alongside the quarry, an eloquent testimony to the futile labour of former inmates.

Next come the shipwrecks. There are at least three recent relics marooned on the rocks of the northern shore. One still drifts and lolls in the swells, constantly changing position, while the detritus of the vessel's interior litters the coastline. Two other substantial wrecks have been pulled out of the water and sit stranded on the shore, speaking volumes about the treacherous nature of the rocks that ring the island.

On the northeastern side of the island, the penguins take over. And there are thousands of the little beggars. Their burrows pock the ground and the fearless creatures constantly criss-cross the road as they waddle from the water to their holes. Since humans are not a common sight here, the penguins are in their element. They throng along the water's edge, standing to attention on the rocks and splashing in the waves, as huge freighters cut through the intervening strait on their way to Cape Town harbour. There are also several WWII outlooks on this part of the island, keeping their empty vigil over the Blouberg channel.

Behind this penguin playground is a substantial gum plantation, the remains of the Cornelia Battery, the island's power station, a refuse plant and the old jail (which held the island's first intake of modern prisoners). An old military observation tower is visible over the tops of the trees. This part of the island was also the location of several leper villages but no evidence of these settlements remains. From here, it is a short stroll back to the harbour and the maximum-security prison.

The island walk only takes a few hours but it incorporates over 500 years of history and a pristine natural environment that really nourishes the soul. If, at some stage, you get the chance to do this walk for yourself, don't hesitate. It will take your breath away.

Final thoughts

When I returned from my short stay on Robben Island, I spent a night in Sea Point before returning to Joburg.

That evening, I stood on the balcony of my friend's flat and looked out over the bay towards the dark bulk of the island. The beacon from the lighthouse blinked on and off and I could see the small cluster of flickering lights from the far-off village. I felt nostalgic and melancholy. I wanted to go back. The island had touched me in a way that I had not expected and I longed to return to its noisy solitude and barren beauty. The words of Johnny Clegg's anthem, 'Asimbonanga', rang in my ears: 'The sea is cold and the sky is grey, looking at the island across the bay. We are all islands, till comes the day, we cross the burning water'. Thankfully, that day has now come and we should all be proud of our national achievement.

And yet, for all its allure, one cannot forget that Robben Island is a place of atrocity. No matter how transcendent it may now appear, it was once a dark and terrible place.

So now, finally, I must try to sum up my feelings about Robben Island. And yet I find this impossible. I fell in love with the peace and beauty of the island but this seems somewhat facile in light of all that has transpired on the rocky little outcrop. I also feel empathy for the many prisoners who were forced to live and die in captivity on the island. Yet this seems trite coming from someone who was lucky enough to have escaped the worst repercussions of apartheid.

All I can say is the Robben Island is unique. It doesn't feel like any other place on Earth. And, unlike the prisoners of years gone by, I can't wait to go back.

The site today

Plans for the future

The Robben Island Museum is currently operating at capacity. Just about every ferry is fully booked and around half a million people visit the island every year. Nevertheless, the museum authorities have some exciting plans in the pipeline that will add value to the experience and improve accessibility to the wonders of Robben Island.

Among the proposals they are currently considering are a guided walking tour around the island (which would be brilliant) and a mountain-bike tour around the island (which would be less brilliant, because cycling makes my bum sore). A new restaurant and even overnight accommodation are also on the cards.

Furthermore, a new exhibition and education centre has just been opened, mainly for school tours, and it is rather ironically located in the old medium-security prison that used to hold the criminals.

However, implementing these new facilities is going to be very difficult indeed. The island's eco-system is very fragile and it contains several endangered species of plants and animals. The local community would also be heavy impacted by a sudden influx of strangers. One can only imagine how the quiet village atmosphere would be shattered by a rowdy group of holidaymakers who want to get drunk and chase the penguins.

Access to the island must therefore be controlled. But what mechanism should be used to determine who gets to go? They could charge high prices, for example, but I firmly reject a purely financial qualification, which effectively makes the island a playground for the rich. High prices would also exclude many South Africans from experiencing this exquisite island, and that would be a shame. The powerful dollars and euros of international visitors easily overwhelm the purchasing power of rand-based travellers, and the number of local tourists is already relatively low.

When I did the bus tour, the guide asked if there were any South Africans on board. Out of 40 people, only two of us put up our hands. The subtle pleasures of Robben Island should therefore remain available to all. This is a tremendous challenge that the museum management must negotiate. Extensive discussions with the various stakeholders are thus underway to establish an equitable system, and one can only hope that the planners get it right.

Robben Island Museum information

Pricing (as of March 2009):

- Adults: R180
- Children (ages 4 – 17): R90
- Special rates are available for schools, educational outings and disadvantaged groups, on application to the education or marketing departments
- Credit cards and cash are the preferred methods of payment. Electronic transfer (EFT) facilities are available. Personal cheques may be accepted, subject to conditions. Travellers cheques are not accepted

Times:

- The primary ferry, *Sikhululekile*, currently departs at 09:00, 11:00, 13:00 and 15:00
- The secondary ferry, *Susan Kruger*, usually departs at 10:00 and 14:00 during the summer season, although these trips are scheduled according to demand
- The Nelson Mandela Gateway is open daily from 07:00 to 17:30
- The Museum is open year-round, including Christmas Day and New Year. It is, however, closed on Workers' Day (1 May)
- Operating times may be extended during peak-season (December and January)
- The tour may be cancelled due to inclement weather and/or rough seas
- The tour takes between 3½ and 4 hours to complete

Advance bookings:

- The tour is always heavily booked. During peak season, around 1,800 visitors a day will visit the island. Advance booking is therefore strongly recommended. It is advised that you book at least three days in advance to avoid disappointment. Always phone ahead to check availability
- Phone bookings must be paid for in advance, either with credit card or by electronic transfer. Cash payments are only accepted at the ticket office in the Gateway building
- Internet bookings are now available. You can book online at: www.webtickets.co.za/robbenisland

The tour includes:

- A return ferry trip across Table Bay to the island
- A 45-minute guided bus tour around the southern part of the island
- A walking tour through the Maximum Security Prison, guided by an ex-political prisoner
- A look at Mandela's cell

Wheelchair access:

- The Gateway is fully accessible for those using a wheelchair, as is the ferry. The prison has a couple of stairs, which can be navigated with a little assistance. People using wheelchairs should give the Museum advance notice so that they can arrange for a bus with a ramp to be available on the island

Other:

- It is recommended that you wear comfortable walking shoes, a hat, sunglasses and sun-protection cream
- Photos and videos may be taken at most places on the island
- Robben Island is a national heritage site and a World Heritage Site. As such, it is forbidden to remove or deface any object. Even stones and shells may not be removed
- The island is a gun-free zone. Before embarkation, all firearms must be handed to a security officer at the Gateway
- Smoking is only permitted at designated areas at the quayside on Robben Island

Contacts:

Advance bookings
Tel: 021-413 4233/7
Fax: 021-418 3736
email: rimbookings@robben-island.org.za
website: www.robben-island.org.za

General info—Nelson Mandela Gateway
Tel: 021-413 4220/1
e-mail: infow@robben-island.org.za

General info—Robben Island
Tel: 021-409 5169
email: infoi@robben-island.org.za

Educational tours
Tel: 021-409 5250
Fax: 021-411 1931
email: educate@robben-island.org.za

Specialized tours/conferences
Tel: 021-409 5182
Fax: 021-411 1934
email: events@robben-island.org.za

Nelson Mandela Gateway Boardroom & Auditorium
Tel: 021-413 4222
email: debram@robben-island.org.za

Memorabilia stores
Tel: 021-413 4223 (Nelson Mandela Gateway)
Tel: 021-409 5103 (on the Island)

Cape Town Tourism information & Robben Island booking office
Tel: 021-405 4500
Fax: 021-405 4524
email: info@tourcapetown.com

References/further reading

- Bloem, Trudie. 1999. *Krotoa-Eva, the woman from Robben Island.* Kwela Books
- Bulpin, T.V. 2001. *Discovering Southern Africa.* Tafelberg Publishers
- Bunting, Brian. 1969. *The Rise of the South African Reich.* Penguin Africa Library (reprinted by IDAF, 1986)
- Cope, John. 1967. *King of the Hottentots.* Howard Timmins
- Deacon, Harriet (editor). 1996. *The Island—a history of Robben Island 1488–1990.* David Philip Publishers and Mayibuye Books
- Fleminger, David. 2005. *Back Roads of the Cape.* Jacana Media
- Forsberg, Annika. *Robben Island for children.* Robben Island Museum Education Department
- Mostert, Noel. 1992. *Frontiers—the epic of South Africa's creation and the tragedy of the Xhosa people.* Pimlico
- National Ports Authority. 1991. *Lighthouses of South Africa*
- Peires, Jeff. 2003. *The Dead Will Arise—Nongqawuse and the great Xhosa Cattle Killing of 1856–7.* Jonathan Ball Publishers
- Sleigh, Dan (translated by André Brink). 2004. *Islands.* Secker and Warburg
- Smith, Charlene. 1997. *Robben Island.* Struik Publishers

Useful websites

- www.robben-island.org.za – official Robben Island Museum website
- www.mayibuye.org – Robben Island-Mayibuye archives, University of the Western Cape
- www.sahistory.org.za – outstanding site that has in-depth information about all aspects of SA history
- www.wikipedia.org – on-line encyclopaedia
- www.tourismcapetown.co.za – official Western Cape and Cape Town tourism site
- www.waterfront.co.za – Victoria and Alfred Waterfront website
- www.freedom.co.za – website about Robben Island's history and ecology
- http://whc.unesco.org – UNESCO World Heritage Centre website
- http://whc.unesco.org/en/statesparties/za – UNESCO World Heritage, South Africa homepage
- www.worldheritagesite.org – World Heritage website
- www.wmf.org – World Monument Fund website
- www.icomos.org – International Council on Monuments and Sites
- www.sahra.org.za – South African Heritage Resource Agency
- www.nhc.org.za – National Heritage Council of South Africa

Index

African National Congress (ANC) 12, 58-61, 68-70
African People's Democratic Union of South Africa 60
Alcatraz 12
Alexander, Neville 61
Amatola Mountains 42
Amnesty International 65
Anglican Church 45, 91
Anglo-Boer War 57
Anglo-Xhosa wars (Frontier wars) 11, 12, 36-42
Anglo-Zulu War 57
Apartheid 56-63, 66, 68-70
Autshumao (Herrie) 21-26, 28, 30
Azanian People's Organization (AZAPO) 60

Baker, Sir Herbert 46, 90
Bam, Fikile 61
Bantu Education Act 67
Basson, Derrick 93
Batavia 22, 28, 32, 34
Bath of Bethesda 47, 83, 99
Bergselaar, Sgt. 99
Berndt, Florrie 33
Biko, Steve 67, 88
Black consciousness 60, 67, 68, 88
Blank, Claas 33
Bloubergstrand 13, 14, 92
Blue slate quarry 83
Bokkeveld Rebellion 43
Bonaparte, Napoleon 33, 34
Boom, Hendrik 21
Botha, Louis 57
Botha, P. W. 68, 69
Boubou 26
British East India Company 17
Bushmen (San) 36, 37, 43

Camps Bay 13, 99
Cape Corps 54
Cape of Good Hope 17, 34
Chainouqua 22
Chapman's Peak 99
Chochoqua 22
Church of the Good Shepherd 13, 46, 49, 83, 90
Church of the Province of South Africa 13
Clegg, Johnny 101
Cooper, Saths, 61
Cornelia Battery 53, 55, 83, 100
Cou, Jan 26
Crosse, Capt. John 16, 18, 19

da Gama, Vasco 15
Daniels, Eddie 61
Dassen Island 16
de Klerk, F. W. 69
De Waal Battery 53, 56, 83, 92
Defiance Campaign 59, 77
Devil's Island 12
Devil's Peak 92
Dlamini, Moses 63
Doman 25-27
Duke of Orange 34
Duncan, Peggy 33
Dutch East India Company (the VOC—Vereenigde Ooste-Indische Kompagnie) 16, 17, 20, 22, 23, 28, 32, 34, 38, 94

Eva see Krotoa

Fire Hill see Minto Hill
Fitzpatrick, Thomas 35
Fong Chung II shipwreck 83, 92, 99
Freedom Charter 86
French Guyana 12
Frontier wars see Anglo-Xhosa wars

Garrison Church *see* Anglican Church
Gogosoa 27
Goldberg, Denis 61
Gorachouqua 20, 22
Goringhaikona *see* Strandlopers
Goringhaiqua 22, 25-27
Graaff-Reinet 37, 62
Grahamstown 37, 39
Great Fish River 36
Great Trek 38
Guru, Tuan 32
Gwala, Harry 61

Hassim, Kader 61
Hector 17, 18
Herrie *see* Autshumao
Hertzog, J. B. 52, 53
Hitler, Adolf 52
Hlubi 43
Howick 60

Indian Congress 60
International Council on Monuments and Sites (ICOMOS) 11, 107
International Union for Conservation of Nature (IUCN) 9
Irish Town 45, 55, 90

Jacobsz, Rijkhaart 33

Ka Isaka Seme, Pixley 58
Kathrada, Ahmed 12, 61
Kayti 41
Khalifa 32, 94
Khoikhoi 12, 14, 16-30, 32, 33, 36-39, 43
Kimberley 57, 62
King George III 34
King James 17
King, Martin Luther 67

Kleynhans brothers 63, 75
Kora (Koranna/wars) 20, 43
kramat 32, 83, 94
Krotoa (Eva) 21, 24, 25, 30, 106

Land Act 57, 58
Langalibalele 43
League of Nations Health Organization 51
Lekota, Mosiuoa 'Terror' 61
Leprosy Repression Act 49
Liberal Party 60
Liliesleaf Farm, Rivonia 60
Lion's Head 92
Llandudno 53
Luthuli, Albert 60, 61

Madiba *see* Mandela, Nelson
Maharaj, Mac 61
Makhanda 39, 41
Malan, D. F. 58
Malcolm X 67
Mamoepa, Ronnie 61
Mandela, Nelson 12, 56, 60, 61, 64-66, 69, 70, 77, 79, 82, 95, 96, 104
Mandela, Winnie 70
Maqoma 41, 42
Masemola, Japhta 78
Mbeki, Govan 61, 63
Mbeki, Thabo 63
Mhala 41, 42
Mhlakaza 41
Mhlaba, Raymond 61
Minto Hill (*also* Fire Hill) 14, 23, 83, 92
Mixed Marriages Act 58, 69
Mkwayi, Wilton 61
Mlambo, Johnson 61, 64
Mlangeni, Andrew 61
Mlanjeni 40, 41
Monomatapa, Kingdom of 28
Montagu, John 43, 44

Moodley, Strini 61
Mothopeng, Zephania 61
Motsoaledi, Elias 61
Moturu, Sheik Sayed Adurohman 32, 94
Muizenberg 34
Murray, John 35, 39, 40
Murray's Bay/Harbour 41, 49, 53, 83, 88

Nair, Billy 61
Namaqua 28
National Liberation Front 60
National Party 55, 58
National Ports Authority 13, 91, 106
Ndlambe 40
New Year's Gift 19, 20
Newgate Prison 18
Ngqika 42
Nongqawuse 40, 41, 106
Norfolk Island 12
Nzima, Sam 67

Oppenheimer, Harry and Bridget 54
Orange Free State 57
Osinghkhimma 27
Ossewa Brandwag 54
Oukamp, Cmdt. 76

Pan-Africanist Congress (PAC) 12, 59-61, 64, 68, 69, 73, 74, 77, 79
Pass Laws 59, 69
Pato 41
Petersen, Hector 67
Pirow, Oswald 52
Plaatjies 48
Pokela, John Nyathi 61
Pollsmoor Prison 69, 96
Population Registration Act 58
Poqo (armed wing of PAC) 59

Pretoria Central Prison 60, 61

Queenstown 57

Rand Daily Mail 73
Red Cross 65
Rivonia Eight/Trial 60, 61, 69, 77
Robbeljaert, Cpl. 31
Robben Island Council 13
Robben Island Mayibuye Archive 86, 107
Robben Island Museum 13, 71, 88, 89, 102-105
Robben Island Village Association (RIVA) 98

San *see* Bushmen
Sandile 42
Schapenjacht 26
Schmidt, Johan 40
Sea Point 13, 99, 101
Sexwale, Tokyo 61
Shaffers, Rev. 80
Sharpeville massacre 59, 61, 74
Signal Hill 52
Simon's Town 53
Sir Lowry's Pass 44
Sisulu, Walter 61, 63
Siyolo 40, 42
Smuts, Jan 52, 53, 55, 58
Smythe, Sir Thomas 17, 18, 20
Sneeuberg Mountains 37
Sobukwe, Robert 12, 59, 61, 62, 83, 90
Sotho 36
South African Native Congress 57
South African Party 52, 58
South African Women's Auxiliary Naval Service (SWANS) 54
South West Africa People's Organization (SWAPO) 12, 60, 61
Soweto uprising 67, 90

Status Campaign (PAC) 77
Stokwe 41
Strandlopers 22, 26
Stuurman, David 39, 40
Suzman, Helen 65
Swartberg Pass 44

Table Bay (*also* Saldania) 13, 17,
    22, 31, 52, 53, 88, 104
Table Mountain 13, 35, 48, 80, 85,
    87, 92, 98
Tambo, Oliver 61
Tefu, Matlakana Philemon 72-80
Theron, warder 76
Thunberg, Carl 31
Toivo ya Toiva, Andimba Herman
    12, 61
Tola 41
Transvaal (ZAR) 57
Treason Trial 58, 59
Trekboers *see* Voortrekkers
Trompetter, Hans 39, 40
Tsfendas, Dimitri 66
Tshwete, Steve 61
Twelve Apostles 99

U-boats 52, 53
Umkhonto we Sizwe (MK, armed
    wing of ANC) 59
United Democratic Front (UDF)
    60
United Nations (UN) 8, 10, 11,
    65, 69
United Nations Economic,
    Scientific and Cultural
    Organization (UNESCO) 8, 9,
    11, 13, 107
Unity Movement 60
University of Cape Town (UCT)
    15
University of the Western Cape
    (UWC) 108
Urban Areas Act 58

Valkenberg Asylum 50
van Meerhof, Pieter 28
van Riebeeck, Jan 15, 20-29,
    31, 55
Van Riebeeck's quarry 55, 83, 99
Venkatrathnam, Sonny 61
Verwoerd, H. F. 58, 59, 66
Victor Verster Prison 70
Victoria & Alfred (V&A)
    Waterfront 14, 84, 85, 107
VOC *see* Dutch East India
    Company
Voortrekkers 36, 57
Vorster, B. J. 68

Wagenaar, Zacharias 31
Werz, Bruno Dr. 15
Wessels, Col. 75
Westfort Hospital 51
Witwatersrand 57
Women's Auxiliary Air Force
    (WAAF) 54
Women's Auxiliary Army Service
    (WAAS) 54
World War II 8, 11, 52, 56, 58,
    89, 90

Xayimpi 41
Xhore 16-20, 22
Xhosa 11, 12, 36-43, 57, 106
Xoxo 41, 42

Zille, warder 76, 77
Zulu 36, 43, 57
Zuma, Jacob 61

INDEX

Acknowledgments

I wish to thank the entire staff of the Robben Island Museum and Nelson Mandela Gateway for making my stay so memorable. I also thank all the Robben Island residents, young and old, for their friendliness and warmth. I thoroughly enjoyed my short stay in your village and am eternally grateful for the time and knowledge that you shared with me. Final thanks go to, as always, to my family and friends—especially the Capetonian crew and the Rosmarins, who always let me stay in their legendary flat for free! And lastly, thanks to Jayne Southern for the proof-reading.

Picture credits

All photographs were taken by David Fleminger.